T0090628

# RAISING
## THE
# WOUNDED

# RAISING
## THE
# WOUNDED

*Grasping for Hope
in the Midst of Despair*

JOHN D. DOUGHLIN

authorHOUSE®

*AuthorHouse™ UK Ltd.*
*1663 Liberty Drive*
*Bloomington, IN 47403 USA*
*www.authorhouse.co.uk*
*Phone: 0800.197.4150*

*© 2014 John D. Doughlin. All rights reserved.*

*The author assumes full responsibility for the accuracy of all facts and quotations as cited in this book.*

*No part of this book may be reproduced, stored in a retrieval system, or transmitted by any means without the written permission of the author.*

*Unless otherwise noted, all Scripture references are from the King James Version.*

*Published by AuthorHouse    10/02/2014*

*ISBN: 978-1-4969-9231-4 (sc)*
*ISBN: 978-1-4969-9232-1 (e)*

*Any people depicted in stock imagery provided by Thinkstock are models, and such images are being used for illustrative purposes only. Certain stock imagery © Thinkstock.*

*This book is printed on acid-free paper.*

*Because of the dynamic nature of the Internet, any web addresses or links contained in this book may have changed since publication and may no longer be valid. The views expressed in this work are solely those of the author and do not necessarily reflect the views of the publisher, and the publisher hereby disclaims any responsibility for them.*

*Texts credited to NKJV are taken from the New King James Version. Copyright © 1982 by Thomas Nelson, Inc. Used by permission. All rights reserved.*

*Scripture quotations marked (NIV) are taken from the HOLY BIBLE, NEW INTERNATIONAL VERSION®. NIV ®. Copyright © 1973, 1978, 1984 by International Bible Society. Used by permission of Zondervan. All rights reserved.*

*Scripture quotations abbreviated AMP are taken from the Amplified® Bible, Copyright © 1954, 1958, 1962, 1964, 1965, 1987 by The Lockman Foundation. Used by permission. (www.Lockman.org)*

*Scripture quotations abbreviated NLT are taken from the Holy Bible, New Living Translation, Copyright ©1996. Used by permission of Tyndale House Publishers, Inc. Wheaton, Illinois 60189. All rights reserved.*

# ACKNOWLEDGEMENTS

Such an achievement as this was not acquired in a vacuum. In reality, I could not have completed this volume without divine inspiration, nor without the assistance of family members, friends and professionals.

I truly express my grateful thanks to the God of Heaven for inspiring me with the many thoughts so that I could minister to you. To complete six chapters in six weeks is a testimony of true divine inspiration. Additionally, I can still hear the voice of my wife echoing in my ears: "May the Lord bless you!" Thank you, Hon!. And then, my son's constant inquiry as to whether or not the book was finished, reminded me that it was overdue. His questions acted as the push-factor to get the manuscript out of hands and on the publisher's desk.

Dir. R. J. Jordan's voice also continued to remind me of the need to dispatch the manuscript to the publisher. Moreover, her tireless efforts in reading the manuscript in an effort to help me clarify my points are invaluable to this project. Thank you, Dr Jordan.

Finally, I realise my indebtedness to the many authors who have already written on the subject. The books and studies, which I consulted, have been of immense value to me. They have stimulated my thinking and broadened my understanding, even though I did not always agree with the views that were expressed. Had the Library staff at Leeds University not aided me in locating some of the articles and books, this project would have been left uncompleted.

# DEDICATION

I dedicate this book to Keisha Andrea Ferrigon, with permission from her husband. Keisha, who was a powerful and talented youth leader, displayed great interest in the welfare of the youth under her care.

This dedication is fitting, in that her local church and others around the country spent time in prayer, trusting that God would restore and heal her. We accepted the divine will when she fell asleep peacefully.

*I thank her for the guidance she provided*
*for our youth, including my son.*

From her Spiritual Guide!

# CONTENTS

# FOREWORD

John D. Doughlin's success might be a surprise for those who knew him as a child with the odds stacked against him. But he believes in miracles and has seen them happened in his own life. He is the author of four books, one of, which chronicles lessons of faith that God wanted to help him understand, to help – undoubtedly – those who would pass through similar valleys.

This book, *Raising the Wounded: Grasping for Hope in the Midst of Despair,* which you have in your hands is undoubtedly one the most useful books you will ever read for helping to bring hope to families and individuals struggling to find healing for their emotional wounds. The author draws on his personal experience as a spiritual mentor to walk with the 'family'. You will learn that answers are not easy to find, but by trusting in God, you can be assured that exposed emotional wounds can be healed.

*Raising the Wounded* also goes beyond just the emotional and physical, as the author applies spiritual bandages to wounds in need of healing. The anger and destructive patterns in the 'family' are evident, but the family remains determined to find solutions. The writer's compassionate approach and skilful interventions have helped significantly in moving the family, step by step, in finding hope.

This volume is truly a remarkable book. A thoroughly gripping story which explores the hurts of open wounds, but it tells the story of what happens when a heart is open to the promise of healing from an all-encompassing God. Strategically, the author has placed biblical texts at the appropriate locations in the family's narrative to demonstrate that *"God heals the broken hearted and binds up their wounds* (Psalms 147:3). This book will be a great resource for any family or individual trying to find a way to "let go and let God". Readers will no doubt find it difficult to put this book, as the author discusses the power of anointing.

**Pastor Ricardo Selman MS, MFT**
**Family Ministries Director**
**East Caribbean Conference of Seventh-day Adventists,**
**BARBADOS WI**

# INTRODUCTION

# Searching For An Escape Route

"Can't you see that the only thing shining on you is your hair? You don't even deserve to live."

These were the piercing and emotionally damaging words Sandra heard from her husband one month after their wedding in 1986. With the honeymoon having ended in a tense and heated argument three weeks earlier, Sandra's husband arrived home from work late one afternoon, exhausted and mentally drained. But the only thing that greeted him was the radio announcer from VCX Radio Station on 90.1 MW. On making his way into the house, he discovered that his wife was in the kitchen.

"Are you now preparing dinner?" Samuel shouted fiercely.

"What does it look like?" his wife replied.

"Can't you see that the only thing shining on you is your hair? You don't even deserve to live."

These dagger-like words were the fuel that lit an emotionally-draining and stressful marriage. Since that evening the domineering, self-conceited Samuel constantly battered his peaceful wife verbally with the same words. Sandra began thinking. *This was not the husband I married. What has taken over him? Is he sick?* But then another thought rushed through her mind. *Are you going to stay and let him treat you like that?* Week by week this thoughtful wife was losing weight. Her mind was wandering daily. Her husband's bitter and inhumane words kept drilling her thoughts. Immediately she shook herself out of the self-absorbing thoughts. Trouble was brewing for her. Does she have the inner strength and faith to live through this ordeal? Will the God of Heaven bring deliverance for her?

The following day, Samuel had not worked for three hours before his house telephone rang.

"Hello!" his wife answered.

"Good morning! Is this Samuel's wife?" the manager on the other end asked.

"Yes."

"I am your husband's manager and am calling to let you know that your husband began acting strange as soon as he came to work this morning. I think he needs to see a doctor urgently. Can you come and accompany him?"

As she placed the receiver down, those fateful words riveted her mind: 'Can't you see that the only thing shining on you is your hair? You don't even deserve to live.' At that moment, she froze with ambivalent thoughts going through her mind. She was caught between two decisions: either to go to her husband's rescue or leave the marriage. Her heart immediately melted with compassion and she dashed off to meet her husband. In the meantime, she was coming to terms with her six-month pregnancy.

Having arrived at Samuel's workplace, his wife placed him in her car, while a work colleague accompanied him. His wife sped along the dual carriageway to the family's doctor. On arriving at the doctor's surgery, Samuel was trembling nervously. The doctor examined him for about ten minutes. Then he posed a number of questions at him: "What is your name? Do you know where you are? What day of the week is today?" By now Samuel was lost in his own world. And then he lost control.

"Who do you think you are?" he shouted at the doctor.

"Mister, you need to calm down," the doctor advised.

On realising that he was becoming more and more hysterical, the doctor administered a tranquilising injection. He immediately called the psychiatric hospital and reported Samuel's behaviour. Meanwhile, Samuel's eyes roared in fire and anger. The doctor shared with Sandra his concerns and alerted her that he will need to be hospitalised for a few weeks. The following days were devastating for Sandra. *Will I have to live through this for the rest of my life? Will I be able to have a happy family? Can my child endure this situation?* She thought. This was the time when this family began to experience open wounds. Will Sandra remain with her domineering husband? Is there a way of escape for her?

The weeks had rushed by speedily. Samuel, having settled down and become more stable, was discharged from hospital. The weeks away from home made him more vocal and disturbing. But on hearing that he was about to become a dad, Sandra hoped that he would be transformed. However, on returning to work, trouble escalated for her. In trying to juggle her studies in social work with working night shifts and taking care of her unborn baby, her body was melting under the pressure. Life is uncertain and unpredictable. Like this family, when we encounter such circumstances, we want to acquire healing for our wounds. Whether it is emotional or physical wounds, we hope that someone would grasp for hope in the midst of despair.

*Raising the Wounded: Grasping for Hope in the Midst of Despair* portrays the dramatic journey of a working class 'family', whose members were living with open emotional, physical and psychological wounds. This volume focuses, not so much on whether or not it is God's will for us to be healed, but on the view that we can request healing, through prayer and anointing, while we may be in anguish from the sting of cancer or from the bitter pain of our emotional difficulties. We would agree that suffering is present in many villages, communities, and various parts of the world. It ranges from hunger and starvation to excruciating sickness. However, when we look at suffering in its various forms, it prevails in human societies and among those of us who are least able at times to help ourselves rise above this suffering. It may be a spiritual problem in our life or it may not be God's will for us to be healed of the particular sickness. Additionally, we may lack the finances or resources to acquire a particular remedy or we may not believe in divine healing through which restoration of our holistic well-being can be achieved.

If we are honest about our lifestyles, we would agree with the perspective offered by William H. Willimon, that "we live in a therapeutic culture where all human problems are reduced to sickness. We want not so much to be saved or changed, but rather to feel better about ourselves."[1] When God's created beings hold such a narrow view of their existence it would seem that we have lost sight of the bigger picture for our total well-being. Some individuals perceive a religious figure mainly as "the therapist who helps evoke spiritually-inclined sentiments in individuals – soothing anxiety, caring for the distressed and healing the maladjusted."[2] But people from all walks of life welcome any good news of a medicine or some other means that would bring a cure for AIDS, cancer or even that disturbing ailment that is present in the body.

Living under these circumstances can create desperation in our hearts, forcing us to clutch at any available support or comfort. Meanwhile, our inner world is in turmoil and we carry a look of urgency in our eyes. Like Sandra, we prayerfully wrestle on our knees because lives are on the verge of being shattered. And when these individuals are people close to us, we push harder to find deliverance. But in spite of the challenges of life, we can draw on our faith and the Word of God.

Desperation creates a passionate thirst and a longing hunger in us. Actually, a thirsty heart personifies the longing that exists in our life, signalling a quest for answers to life's haunting questions. This inner thirst sits squarely in the context of family-especially a wounded family. Family signifies the existence of comfort, love, peace and protection. It is in this social setting that we gain a glimpse of God in action, in that we learn about Him, we learn to pray, see his caring acts, feel His grace extended to unworthy individuals and experience punishment when necessary. Family helps us with our spiritual journey even though we have to face the twists and turns.

This volume, *Raising the Wounded: Grasping for Hope in the midst of Despair,* is aimed at youth and young adults who have been grappling desperately with emotional, physical and psychological problems in their lives. The mind rages with various questions, our thoughts are bombarded with painful events from the past and present and we seem powerless to shake the hurt and rise above the mental anguish. Individuals such as you and me live with physical ailments and we carry around the perspective that nothing can be done about our situation. But where is God when we are hurting? How can the vulnerable and the weak find comfort during their difficult times? This volume has been written to assist you in understanding that you can request divine healing for your ailments even when there are no medical solutions.

Unlike most volumes on the subject of healing, *Raising the Wounded* is unique, in that, it addresses, from an academic and biblical perspective, the private-public and invitational-uninvitational tensions in relation to conducting anointing services for divine healing. In particular, this book will encourage and inspire you powerfully to embark on a devoted prayer life, a vital element of the Christian journey which has empowered my personal life and ministry. Personally, engaging in intercessory prayer has kept me focused and has anchored my self esteem.

In *Raising the Wounded,* community responsibility is the major thematic thread that runs throughout the pages. It is a fact that each of us belongs to a community: ethnic, religious, professional or geographical. How useful is community responsibility to my personal development? Can community responsibility make an impact in our lives? Such questions are addressed in this dramatic and suspense volume. When you embark on travelling through the upcoming pages, you will encounter sub themes such as patience, comforting the wounded, determination and courage. More importantly, when one's community reaches out to its members, using various forms of Christian pastoral care such as anointing, prayer, pastoral and psychiatric counselling and visitation, we come face to face with the grace and caring acts of the Divine One.

At a time in our world's history when there are economic and financial disasters, *Raising the Wounded* demonstrates how we can find release from those debilitating problems we encounter. Families, church leaders and Christian pastoral carers will find this volume helpful in knowing how to guide individuals through difficult problems, be they emotional or psychological. Knowing that God has promised to bestow His blessings on us, we are confronted with various questions: Is God's care for us manifested through community responsibility? How can the weak and the marginalised find relief even though resources are scarce? And How long does the divine clock take to turn?

Although I try to ensure that this book is not too academic, I hold the assumption that the gift of healing prevailed throughout biblical times and the results of healing by anointing reveal God's divine will. Additionally, since healing, forgiveness, reconciliation and restoration are integral to the Gospel, prayer has its proper place alongside the act of anointing. In fact, praying for healing should be taken seriously and be seen as an effective and powerful spiritual discipline.

I also need to offer a disclaimer in introducing this book. Although the events are substantial, all the names, members of the different 'families', dates and geographical locations are fictitious. The pseudonyms have been used, however, on recognising that the events can be the experiences of many families, we seek not to belittle your experience. How can we respond to the desperate pleas of those around us? Have you heard the desperate pleas of the hurting and the wounded? While you prayerfully read this volume, take some time to focus on the *Thoughts for Action* and *Moments of Surrender* sections. It is here that you can reflect on the powerful display of God's grace, be aided in applying the insights to your own life, and thus, acquire the help that you may need for your personal journey. May you find comfort and experience the Hand of God in your own family as you turn the pages of this dramatic story.

# PROLOGUE

Distressing! Horrifying! Shocking! These are some of the reactions to the fatal accident, in the late summer of 1997, of the Princess of Wales, who was often portrayed as 'the people's princess'. After leaving a French hotel in Paris in her black Mercedes-Benz, the popular British Princess, along with her body guard and other companions left the scene of celebration and travelled through a French tunnel.

With photographers behind her, the Mercedes collided in the tunnel and the Princess gravely suffered serious injuries. The impact of the crash reduced the car to a pile of wreckage. In that rubble, the casualties and fatalities lay helpless and critical. The death sparked national, regional and international reactions, elicited global grief and etched sorrow on the hearts of families for years.

A similar incident occurred a few years later. Mrs. Bruce, a mother-of-seven was busy preparing lunch for a group of church members in late autumn 1998. The mid-day service at Mount Vale Community Church in South-West England had finished. Soon after, the congregants descended into the youth hall to savour the delicious meal that the well-organised, efficient and hospitable mother had prepared. Although no snow rained from the sky, an extra-ordinary freezing breeze blew across the church yard. The dishes, of various shapes and sizes which were filled with delicious food, lay on the long tables in the youth hall. As the queue began to stretch, Mrs. Bruce and her team perspired immensely in an effort to cater to the hunger needs of the waiting crowd.

In the crowd, a mobile phone rang and Julian answered it immediately. The voice on the other end relayed some news to the fun-loving and jovial teenager, who immediately rushed over to his mother and spilled the news in his innocence. Mrs. Bruce, being told that three of her children had died in an accident, collapsed under the weight of grief. She never recovered.

"Oh, my children have gone! My children! My children!" she wailed sorrowfully.

Sandra, one of her closest friends who were nearby, grabbed her from crashing to the floor. In the meantime, her mother and father swamped her as the tears flowed from their eyes. Two of Mrs. Bruce's other children, Jane and Yolanda, who were also present, collapsed beside their mother and grandparents.

Nelly, Mrs. Bruce's power-wielding sister, despatched her car to the front entrance of the church so that her sister could be taken home. With tears of grief streaming down her cheeks, she resisted:

"I want to see my children. They are all gone."

"Here, take this glass of water," the thoughtful Sandra replied.

It was impossible at that time because the children, along with another friend, had journeyed to a north-western Spanish city to be with friends for the weekend. While driving on the wet roads, the car apparently skidded sideways and ended in a head-on collision. The car in which these children were travelling was left in a pile of rubble, with the bodies lying listless at the scene. It was impossible to prevent the car crossing over the other side since there were no crash barriers.

The days ahead were painful, difficult and burdensome. The mother-of-seven was too weak to face the reality. Nelly and her husband, Patrick, volunteered to travel to the mainland country, south of the Channel, to retrieve the remains and return with them. On realizing that the accident was too gruesome, Nelly decided that it would be best for her sister not to be near the caskets. This decision caused great confusion among the family members and relatives, to the point, that a sharp rift was created between

Nelly's and her sister's family. Nelly's children hardly, if at all, associated with their cousins, even when they came to church.

A few weeks later, the funeral took place. The mourning mother arrived at the packed church dressed in black and her face covered with a veil. Scores of people were present to show their respect for their three friends who touched the lives of people all over their community. With the tears dripping from her tired eyes, she screamed:

"Let me see them for the last."

Her sister, Nelly, was keeping a close watch on her and on hearing her request, guided her, with help, away from the caskets and through the side entrance. Every effort was made to ensure that Mrs. Bruce did not see her children, even though they lay in state at the church's entrance, thus robbing her of emotional closure.

As time rushed by, the Bruce's family continued to mourn deeply, while receiving great support from other family members, both in England and from the Caribbean. Importantly, Sandra's three daughters, Patricia age 17, Janice age 13 and Judith age 5, became very close to the Bruce's children and frequented their house on many occasions. During the days and months afterwards, through various social events, Jane, Julian and Yolanda attracted other friends, namely Alex and Curtis among others. Being young and vibrant, they often held nights of fun and games in the church's youth centre and at other people's homes.

It was at one of these social events, that Cynthia, the mother of six-year old Benin, and her friend, Sandra, met a trainee student. It was after a few discussions with him, that the young people eventually recommended him to Sophia as a suitable person to co-ordinate the Tuesday night bible discussion sessions. In fact, the young people from this local congregation were entertaining a number of strange biblical views which were contrary to the mainstream beliefs of the denominational church. Soon after being recommended, the potential bible studies co-ordinator was asked to set up the first Tuesday night bible discussion session. And then, it happened.

One Tuesday evening after a bible study session, Sandra, in discussing a number of issues with the co-ordinator, made him aware of her eldest daughter's problems with Tinnitus, her bitterness and deep-seated anger and the distressful marital difficulties she was having with Samuel, her domineering husband, who she had been married to for seventeen years. He felt uneasy about taking on the hurting mother's issues seeing that he had not yet completed his training. In order to find help, he recommended Sharon. Apart from these threatening situations, the other two daughters Janice and Judith were experiencing physical and psychological difficulties, yet there seemed to be no relief. And in the midst of these struggles, these three girls were kept away from school for a protracted period.

Mrs. Bruce's children had a great interest in studying biblical topics and at times, displayed their determination in what they believe. However, on learning about a special weekend prayer programme, they eagerly encouraged Sandra's children and their other friends to attend. It was at this programme that Sandra's eldest daughter, Patricia, experienced a transformation in her life through the power of prayer.

The months sped by, with Mrs. Bruce completely dressed in black almost every day. Coupled with her mournful clothing, was the inner and outer grief that stuck to her like glue. There was still that craving desire to see her children. To ease the grieving process, professional Christian counsellors, grief counsellors and psychotherapists were provided to help the traumatised family members and other church members. There were small-group sessions and one-to-one sessions with relatives, family members and church members. But in spite of the many sessions that were organized, the deaths of the children dealt a sharp, irreparable emotional blow to the now mother-of-four.

# 1

# Open Wounds Hurt

About two billion people in our contemporary world suffer from Hepatitis B. Fifty to sixty million people worldwide have vitiligo. Twenty million Americans have kidney disease. British cancer researchers reveal that some 45 000 women and about 277 men in the United Kingdom have been diagnosed with breast cancer in 2007.[3] There is no doubt, we, who have been affected harshly by various types of diseases, attempt to find healing. Our eager desire to get rid of ailments and sickness causes many individuals to become desperate. The yearning for relief forces many of us to pay large sums of money. Why? To get treatment from the best and most experienced medical specialists. Many pursue renowned consultants. Others check in at highly rated medical centres and prestigious private hospitals.

Our hope for better health and complete healing drives us to take inter-city trips and glide across the Atlantic on this all-time human quest. Samuele Bacchiocchi, in his book, *Divine Rest for Human Restlessness,* rightly asserts that "the ability of modern science to solve what past generations regarded as unsolvable problems had led many to put their faith in human resources rather than divine providence."[4] And that's why some of us even meddle with alternative medicine, and pull out the popular traditional home-made remedies. "Who is the best doctor that can treat my illness?" "How good is your doctor?" and "What did you use to cure your sickness?" are popular questions that people pose to each other. Why? There is that hope of finding our heart's desire. "Yet scientific evidence is mounting that religious affiliation, practice, and related life-styles are conducive to greater longevity, reduced disease, better health and greater life satisfaction." [5]

As we come to grips with the devastation that result from the sickness in our home, community, country and all around the world, hurting individuals continue to pose pointed and purposeful questions: How can I gain healing? Where is this powerful God that I have been hearing about? Our concern for the well-being of others, along with ourselves, provokes us to search frantically. We search intensely for something, beyond the ordinary, which brings the much needed relief. It is true that open wounds hurt profoundly. How can we find long-lasting relief for the taxing emotional and physical ailments that riddle our bodies?

This was the yearning concern of thirty-eight year old Sandra, a hard-working trainee social worker, and her three beautiful daughters, whom I met around July that year. I was totally wrapped up and engrossed in preparations for my postgraduate studies, while living in a sub-urban county. Patricia, the eldest of the three, was suffering from 'catastrophic' subjective Tinnitus. This slim, dark-skinned teenager was determined, well-poised and unusually tall. The phenomenon that gripped her is a condition that interferes with your sleep, disturbs quiet activities, negatively impacts your relationship with others around you and prevents you from engaging in normal daily activities. This high-frequency hiss or buzz occurs continuously and irritates you, to the point that you are less able to cope with different types of activity that were previously normal for you- such as listening to inspiring music and conducting a normal conversation with friends and family members. This condition occurs at any age, but mainly with those who have been exposed to loud noise. [6] Patricia was one of these children. She loves to listen to all types of music on her iPod. Since being diagnosed with this symptomatic condition, she had been absent from school for a two days per week for a year.

Apart from his physical ailment, Patricia had been storing bitterness and boiling anger in her mind ever since her dad had told her that he could not afford to give her spending money to go shopping with her friends. At age seventeen, this intelligent and focused teenager, who was preparing for GCSEs, felt deprived, unloved and treated like a child-minder because she was expected to pick up Judith, her little sister, from school on evenings. The emotional tension raging in her mind along with the impact of the catastrophic Tinnitus disturbed Patricia greatly. No doubt this intense battle was beyond her will power. She was living with open wounds.

Some of us carry open wounds, be they internal or external. But when we consider external wounds which may be abrasions, avulsions, incisions, lacerations or punctures, we must agree that they need bandages. It's wound therapy that aid in the healing process. As we clean the bloody wound, cut away the dangling dead skin, seal the wound with stitches, and dress it, we remove foreign particles and prevent external matter such as dry blood, dust and twigs from interfering with the healing process. It's through this therapeutic process that our wonderfully-made body uses its natural resources to heal such wounds. It's very probable that our external wounds can bring about internal ones. Such wounds can be psychological, mental, emotional or spiritual. These are complex and that's where the professional is needed even more. It could be a psychiatrist, psychotherapist or a vicar. *How can we handle our open wounds? To whom can we turn with our open wounds?* Such was the worrying plight of Sandra and her children.

Meanwhile, Janice, having lost three close friends through a devastating car accident in another country south of the channel, seemed not to have experienced any closure. The indescribable deaths created inner turmoil for her. This medium height impulsive teenager was also angry with her dad who continuously objected to her visiting the shopping centres with her friends. Along with these, she was also emotionally hurt by her sister's problems. She often expressed great empathy towards her older sister as she assisted her mum at home. Along with these situations, her slightly mentally unstable dad, Samuel, a forty-year old driver continued to add salt to Sandra's open wounds by constantly expressing negative views about the children's illnesses. The emotionally-tensed home contributed to Janice's psychological distress becoming intensified, thus leading her to attend a number of sessions with a social worker and a psychologist. As time rushed by, the sullen, melancholy thirteen-year old Janice was recommended for foster care, based on the reports from the professionals. The devastating foster process created a wide chasm in this family that has never been filled.

At age five, Judith, the last of the children in this family, had a speech defect. Since it needed weekly professional intervention, mum had to accompany her to the speech therapist on her off day. To add to her problems, she suffered a bad burn with hot water. One morning, her mum, being tired from working a long shift, had half-filled the bath tub with hot water and turned away to retrieve something from a cupboard. Before she could locate the item, the chubby, inquisitive Judith was screaming. Mum, dad and the other sisters rushed into the bathroom. The skin was peeling off Judith's hands, feet and face. Dad rushed to dial 999, while mum had to abort her morning bath, re-dress and prepare to accompany little Judith to the accident and emergency section of South General Hospital. The accident forced Judith to be absent also from school. And mum had to miss a few days from her training, causing her studies to be extended longer than she had anticipated.

Whenever I looked around for this family at the morning church services, they were nowhere to be seen- at least not in the main worship area. We eventually would meet late on afternoons. It's then that I would catch up with the harsh realities of this family's weekly struggles. One day, while I was spear-heading a youth social event in the park near Mount Vale Community Church, it happened. Young people like Alex, Curtis, Jane, her brother Julian and her sister, Yolanda, were up to their necks in laughter. The thoughts they shared drew long streaks of tears from Julian and Yolanda. Some of the others were moved uncontrollably. They fell to the ground, rolling up on the grass. A few other young people were caught up with the games such as 'musical chairs'. Others were on the sidelines chatting longer than radio announcers. They were all aware of this family's issues, but did not hear Sandra's pain. It was at this time that Mum vocalised her desperation with that fateful question:

"Do you think Patricia will ever be able to hear well again?"

"What do you mean?" I inquired, a bit struck.

"Do you know that she keeps getting this buzzing in her ears?" with a somewhat painful look on her slender face.

"I didn't know," I replied rather reservedly.

"Do you know of anyone who can help? The doctor is saying it may need operation. Because it is severe, they say there is no guarantee that it will stop. But she doesn't want to go for the operation. Plus she is having some emotional problems that are difficult."

Was this sheer care and concern emerging? Was she displaying personal responsibility? Did her questions simply signal moral support? The questions from mum seem legitimate, rightly so, since human beings have the privilege of experiencing healing for the sicknesses that riddle their bodies. So what is the divine plan in the midst of sickness which afflicts people throughout our beautiful and resource-filled planet? Should we accept our illness as the ultimate fate in this life? How can people be relieved of the suffering which ailments bring? Whose responsibility is it to care for the sick? I was stunned, and lost for words. I was paralysed with silence. I did not know what to say or how to respond to this hurting mum. Nevertheless, the question that plagued my mind as I empathised with this family is: How will Sandra obtain total liberation which she desperately desires from these physical and psychological pressures?

The days sped by hurriedly. Yet this wonderful family was eager to participate in all of the exciting church activities among other events. But the girls' health problems curtailed their movements. Patricia found it difficult to sleep at night because of the constant hissing in her ears. Consequently, she could hardly rise early on mornings. And when she joins the other family members down stairs for breakfast, she is still drowsy. As a result, she missed out on many early morning church sessions such as youth bible studies and worship. Sandra, with her meagre financial resources supported her children wholeheartedly, ensuring that they could still attend the afternoon service. Meanwhile, she was scouting around zealously for pastors to provide the urgent relief. Her strong faith in the God of Heaven propelled her to keep searching ardently for reprieve and trusting wholeheartedly in divine power.

From a Christian worldview, the act of creation provided a perfect environment where Adam and Eve, the first human beings, lived peacefully and happily for a short time without being concerned with illness. We would agree that God's creation was absolutely complete and perfect, based on the account in the Holy Scriptures.[7] In Genesis 2, the writer of this first pentateuchal book alerts us to the Divine's intentions for mankind's health. It is from here that we become aware that He "made every tree grow that is pleasant to the sight and good for food" (v.9). The setting created there, suggests that "For all time, Eden became man's highest concept of earthly excellence.[8] Ellen G. White explains that "The Lord was pleased with this last and noblest of all His creatures, and designed that he should be the perfect inhabitant of a perfect world." [9] How then do we make sense of this desired perfect environment and prevailing personal sickness? Can the community-neighbours or even religious, around us express compassion towards individuals with exposed wounds? The way our community responds to our hurts and gruelling pain determine, to a point, how well we progress.

Sometime later, my family and I chatted with Sandra as we were on our way to spend the evening at Cynthia, one of Sandra's friends. The sun was deliberately attempting to peep out beyond the heavy mist and slightly cloudy sky. A strong Western breeze was gliding its way over our heads. At the same time, this strong whistling wind attempted to push us powerfully along the pavement where we were strolling. Having arrived, we saw Cynthia standing in the doorway. They greeted us and then we made our way into the well-perfumed house. It would appear that they were anticipating our company. However, my wife, Maria, became engrossed with Cynthia and her son, Benjamin. Meanwhile, Sandra, with pain and desperation etched on her face, shared openly with me:

"I wish I could get help especially for Patricia. Her hearing is slightly affected, but her emotional difficulties are still problematic."

"I don't know what to do. I guess we will have to live like this," she replied with an air of resignation.

"Don't fear. There's always a way out," I finally added.

"Can something be done? Do you know where I can get help?" she asked, with a smile and a bright ray of hope encircling her face.

The conversation signalled a plea for help, but I did not feel that I was equipped to help her. Neither did I feel that I had reached the stage in my training that I could take on such a massive spiritual challenge. As I reflect on her cry for help, I could not help but realize that there must be a divine desire for this family to experience complete restoration. I thought for a moment that this needed investigating.

Having set out to engage in extensive research on the topic, I noticed in Genesis, the first biblical book, the writer informs us that after each day's creative work of earthly creatures and plants, "God saw that it was good" (Genesis 1:3, 10, 12, 17). Furthermore, F. Martin points out that "healing, the restoration of life, is always the work of Yahweh."[10] Arguably, it can be concluded that the Divine Creator intended to provide a perfect, healthy environment for the first human beings, and by extension, for us today.

We also recognise from the Holy Scriptures that "The tree of life was also in the midst of the garden [of Eden]" (Genesis 2:9b). Such a source of life, indeed, demonstrates the Creator's care about life and therefore, encourages us to desire, not only a long life on earth, but also everlasting life. Moreover, this type of provision also highlights the divine interest in the life span of human beings, with the view that they should live eternally. Indeed, the Hebrew word *hachayyim* for 'life' aids our understanding of the permanence of life. This word in its plural form suggests that 'the tree of life' which was placed in the Garden of Eden, would ensure that mankind's

7

lifespan was continuous. Even Francis Nichol observes that "God had endowed the tree with supernatural virtue. Its fruit being an antidote for death and its leaves for the sustaining of life and immortality, men would continue to live just so long as they should eat of it" and "that life would be obtained or preserved through the use of its fruit."[11] Such a descriptive insight gives us a glimpse of the Divine One's care towards us. It highlights how God had placed this tree in man's view with intent.

The concept of living eternally is captured in the divine instructions to Adam, the first man: "You may freely eat of every tree of the garden; But of the tree of the knowledge of good and evil and blessing and calamity you shall not eat, for in the day that you eat of it you shall surely die" (Genesis 2:16-17, AMP). Clearly, the intention for living eternally was evident from God's reaction to the couple's disobedience, seeing that the Creator did not want the now sinful individuals [Adam and Eve] to "put out his hand and take also of the tree of life, and eat and live forever" (Genesis 3:22). Such scriptural references pinpoint the divine purpose for mankind's continuous earthly existence.

After Adam and Eve disobeyed God's directives in Genesis 2:16-17: "Of every tree of the garden you may freely eat; but of the tree of the knowledge of good and evil you shall not eat, for in the day that you eat of it you shall surely die" sin affected every aspect of the human life, thus leading to sickness and ultimately, to death. However, Yahweh set up a theocracy through which He led the Hebrew nation of Israel. And He spoke through various selected leaders such as Abraham and Moses. Through them, He made the Israelites aware that He was still interested in their total well-being by declaring that "If you diligently heed the voice of the LORD your God and do what is right in His sight, give ear to His commandments and keep all His statutes, I will put none of the diseases on you which I have brought on the Egyptians. For I am the Lord who heals [*rapa*] you" (Exodus. 15:26). [12]

We see how the Holy Scripture paints God's interest in willing to restore the human race to complete health. Indeed, we cannot help but think that this is true for Sandra and her children. Although Patricia's illness was the more severe, Jenny was experiencing emotional struggles. Their health issues were demanding most of Sandra's precious time and hard-earned cash. Janice, the impulsive outspoken short-fused teenager was battling with emotional distress and seemed to be struggling as much as Patricia.

"I couldn't send Janice to school today," she shared with us.

"How comes?" I asked.

"She is not doing well. The psychologist and social worker came to see us today," she added.

"And what's the news?"

"It's going to take time," she replied.

Janice's emotional issues impacted on her interpersonal relationships at school with teachers and the children. At church, it was smooth, but at home, it was too stormy with her dad. In reality, the three girls wished on a few occasions that he was out of their lives- in the grave, actually dead. Janice, the boldest of the children, offloaded her thoughts on others without taking the consequences into consideration. Was it boldness or a display of behavioural issues?

"I am trying to cope, mummy," Janice interjected, "but you don't think so. You want me out of your life that's why you agree to let me be adopted. I wish I wasn't born."

"Don't say that. I know you are," mum urged, "but you should make a little more effort," Sandra replied, stroking her second daughter comfortingly and clinging closely to her as if not wanting to lose her.

When I ponder on the struggles of this family, I remember the event in the largest and most remote Chinese city in the western half of this densely populated Republic, police marched a man in handcuffs into a courtroom. His family had been convinced beyond a shadow of a doubt that he was probably dead. But when he emerged he was like a man returning from the grave. For months, they had been hounding the prison officials, begging for any news of him. They searched computer records and spoke to prison staff, desperate for any sign that this community leader was still alive. Nobody had any record of him. He had disappeared into the murky justice system, where more people are executed every year than in the rest of the world combined. "My son had vanished and I thought he was killed, said his 75-year-old mother, in the first full-length interview given by the man's family members since his arrest in 2006.

Sometime in August 2007, unexpectedly, there was news of a trial date in this city in the far west. The elderly and frail mother, along with 19 other relatives, attended the trial. They watched with amazement as two policemen brought their beloved son, brother and cousin into the room. "My heart was pounding," his mother said. But her joy was short-lived. A few hours later, her son testified that his captors had threatened to have him "buried alive if he refused to sign a confession." She collapsed, sobbing, and had to be helped out of the courtroom by two relatives. "When I heard his words, I was afraid we would lose him," the tearful mum admitted.

That's how we feel at times. There is that feeling of fear that we will lose our loved ones to the ravages of the sickness that has gripped them so long. That is why we hunger for the cure to any disease that attacks our bodies and curtails our treasured and habitual daily routine. Like Sandra and her family, we search frantically, hoping to stumble upon that formula or activity that would improve our emotional, physical and spiritual well-being. But in Exodus 23:26, the Divine Word reminds us of a powerful promise: "So you shall serve the LORD your God, and He will bless your bread and your water. And I will take sickness away from the midst of you." Here we find further reference of the Divine One declaring Himself as Healer, thus demonstrating His plan to provide peace and perfect health for mankind. Indeed, the Divine One is all powerful, a fact that we can safely abide in, knowing that healing can be ours. In essence, we see Him clearly making a promise to bring divine healing to the inhabitants of ancient Israel, and by extension, to anyone who acknowledges Him as Creator in our contemporary world.

Taking a look at the first New Testament book, the Gospel of St. Matthew, the writer points out that during His extensive journeys, "Jesus went throughout Galilee, teaching in their synagogues, preaching the good news of the kingdom, and healing every disease and sickness among the people" (St. Matthew 4:23, NIV). From the Greek text, we get a sense that as Jesus, The Great Teacher, cured, *therapeuo,* various kinds of illnesses, He was sending the message, emphatically, that this particular disease should not have existed in the first place. Further to this general description, Matthew, the Gospel writer, portrays Jesus as having clear intentions of relieving the helpless sick of their suffering by referring to His extensive healing ministry at least three other times.[13] In fact, Ross P. Scherer convincingly argues that "spiritually, however, Jesus and the New Testament authors saw physical and spiritual wellness as so intertwined that, for optimal healthiness, individuals had to have right intentions [*motives*] and relations towards both God and their fellows ("neighbors")."[14] It is from this perspective that we understand Christ's intentions also for us as we exist in a contemporary world where diseases of every imaginable kind emerge.

In fact, the healing events were played out when Jesus publicly rebuked many demons. He also privately removed blindness from a visually impaired individual. Additionally, he publicly restored the dead to life. But Jesus is concerned with individuals' ultimate restoration, irrespective of whether the healing takes place in private or public settings. Moreover, while some urgently invited Jesus to heal them, others were too frail to even think about extending an invitation. God's act of caring for us is also expressed in Him healing our open wounds, and surpasses the private-public tension and invitation-non-invitation debate.

In searching for something in me that could help this family, I asked, "How are you managing, girl?"

"Well, I am working night shifts at a home for people with disability to keep things going. This gives me enough time in the day to be with the girls. And I get more money working nights as a support worker anyhow. Plus I have to go to university three days a week," she informed me.

"We are here for you. Don't forget," I re-assured Sandra.

"I have to do it this way, so that I can have money coming in," she conceded.

"And we have to lock up the house at night and stay 'til you come home in the morning cause my father is never around at night," Janice boldly added.

"An-nnd you hi-iiide," Judith added with difficulty.

"Look who's talking. Scary cat! Even the shadow of the doors frightens you at night," Judith attacked fearlessly, but smiling.

What is comforting is that Scripture provides further evidence to indicate God's interest in our health. In 3 John 2, the writer admonishes: "Beloved, I pray that you may prosper in every way and [that your body] may keep well, *hugiaino*, even as your soul keeps well and prospers" (AMP). Here, prayer is made for our well-being, in at least two areas of our lives: physical and spiritual health. The biblical writer's desire points out the need for individuals to be sound in health, in the same way that they are spiritually whole.

We grasp a glimpse of God's desire for man's well-being. We also discover that God has always had our perfect health in mind, to the extent that eternal life was God's plan for human beings. We have seen that after the Fall of Adam and Eve, and even as Jesus engaged in the work of redeeming individuals by dying at Calvary, the eagerness to have people living as perfectly healthy beings continued to emerge.

In returning to this family's ordeal, the girls' conditions were draining their mother emotionally like a suction pump emptying a water-well. Her face was wearing a mask of tiredness. Her physically tired body was shouting for rest. Going to classes at the university during the day and rushing to nights shifts were taking their toll on her. And to add to her wounds, she often heard her husband's voice battering her mind: 'Can't you see that the only thing shining on you is your hair? You don't even deserve to live.' It was evident that her internal wounds were aching agonisingly.

"Janice is due to return to school in a few weeks time based on the reports from the social worker and the psychologist," mum reminded me, "plus she has been put on the list for foster care."

"How comes? What has been...?" I probed.

I hadn't finished posing my question, when Janice barged into the room.

"I don't want to go with those people! Why do I have to leave my home? They are all the same! I hate everyone," Janice shouted, as she stormed out of the room in tears.

There can be no doubt in our minds that God, the Creator, placed the first human being in Eden's Garden to live continuously and in perfect health. And so we see that the God of Heaven, indeed, cares about our emotional, physical, psychological and spiritual wounds. Certainly open wounds hurt and need a healing touch. From where can we find such a touch? Should this touch be human? Divine? Or a combination of both? Undeniably, the community, where the believer expresses his/her faith in divine power, is the place where the Divine One reveals His grace. Christ is not bound by public or private settings as He soothes our pain and brings restoration to us. His ultimate goal is to redeem us even though we reside in a world infected with various kinds of diseases that are beyond our invention ability.

**Thoughts for Action** *[Jot down your responses]*

- What wounds are you carrying at present/ or did you have in the past?

- Are/Were they exposed or hidden? And are/were they internal or external wounds?

- How have you been/were you able to address such wounds?

- Describe the community to which you are closely connected, be it religious or professional?

- What resources did you have to help you with your healing process?

**Moments of Surrender**

- Is there a past experience with which you are in need of help? If writing it out would help, feel free to take you time and do just that here.

- Take some time to reach out to the God of Heaven by openly sharing the details with Him at this moment.

# 2

# Facing Our Open Wounds

A decade ago a group of passionate, eager and committed young people and I were conducting an intensive prayer service at Lannie's home. Our motivation to have this prayer session came from our lack of personal finances and educational struggles. While living in this Yorkshire rural area, we were bombarded with huge unpaid bills, severe family problems and poor academic grades. As we huddled together in tears, praying for and ministering to each other with various biblical texts, the telephone rang. Lannie, the owner of the house, rushed for the receiver and wiping the tears from her tired eyes, said,

"Hello,"

The caller wanted to speak with someone else.

"One minute. The phone is for you," she replied, handing me the receiver.

It was Jean.

"Dad was just taken to hospital. Please pray for him," she informed me in a tearful manner.

It was disturbing and heart-wrenching news. I dropped the receiver. Immediately, the tears gushed down my checks. Joan came over and hugged me. And then I let it out.

"Jean asked us to prayer right now for her dad. He was just rushed to hospital," I reported.

This was somewhat perplexing and amazing. *Do I have the power to pray for dad's healing? Why didn't she call our pastor?* I thought.

It was a similar situation with Sandra, who was hoping within her heart that someone like me could help her. The support, which mum provided for the girls, was squeezing the life out of her already tired body. Although her obsessive husband, Samuel, left for work around 8:00 a.m during week days, his presence was becoming more and more detrimental to the girls' health. His emotional outburst on his wife continued. His words were like an automatically playing CD: 'Can't you see that the only thing shining on you is your hair? You don't even deserve to live.'

"Dad, can I have some money?" Janice asked.

"Why? Where do you want to go now?" dad demanded.

"Town," Janice replied.

"You can't go to school, but you can walk around in town. Don't leave here." Dad shouted.

The fatherly support was minimal, yet her father was exacting. Added to this, Patricia was expected to accompany Judith on her way to school. Nevertheless, as the days passed by, Patricia had to face up to her own wounds.

Actually, her wounds dictated to her. They decided what she listened to, what time she go to sleep, which activities she engaged in, how conversations with other people proceeded and how loud her music should be. But how do we face our own wounds? It is important to admit and acknowledge the existence of a wound when it occurs. When this is done, half of the healing process has begun. To do otherwise is to engage in denial, a psychological defence mechanism that can negatively impact on the healing process. Nevertheless, the human heart reaches out for divine help. But all too often, we are encouraged to exercise the faith that we have, while waiting on divine power to accomplish a change in our lives. It is cases like these that we cannot rush because the Divine One moves at His own pace and in His own time. Yet He is aware of our dire situations and is poised to respond immediately.

It was a wintry December Saturday evening. We were sitting in the living room at Cynthia's home, while Yolanda was playing with Benjamin, Cynthia's six-year old son. There were smooth fluffy toys of all colours in a corner. The shiny glass-top centre table was well decorated with many beautiful family pictures. A tall oval lamp, with a lilac shade, poised in a corner, was letting off a dim light. By now Janice had returned and was apologising to her mum.

"I am sorry mummy. I didn't mean to do that. I am afraid to be adopted," she admitted, dropping into a sofa.

Facing our wounds can be like standing before a mirror. As our eyes peer into the inner person, we experience ambivalent feelings about what pops up. Life can be tough at times. Our journey can bring wounds with it. And we must acknowledge them on face value in order to move on with our journey. The unexpected image that appears challenges us. Here we are moved to rely on our resources, be their spiritual or natural, to aid us in facing the wounds. In particular, many of us are connected to communities of individuals, who can be shoulders to lean on and hands to soothe our pain. Our hearts need to reach out to our communities as they care for the weak, the disadvantaged and the injured. What joy it is to be part of such responsible communities!

Having returned, Janice stared at her mum, as if to say, 'can't you find someone to help us?' Janice was definitely tired emotionally. The thought of being fostered weighed heavily on her mind. She was about to be ripped away from her family forever. Would she be able to cope? Is she blaming her mother for allowing her to be sent to a foster home? She tried to control her behaviour but there was that burden. Her emotional state gnawed at her behaviour week by week. Mum cuddled her even closer, as if to re-assure her that she still loved her. As she interacted with her friends, it became more and more excruciating. While the emotionally distressed daughter was aware of her problem, she did not have the inner strength to face her open wounds. Such is the case with many of us who also have uncovered wounds. In order to face up to our wounds we must be fortified with emotional strength and be resolved in our hearts that we want to move beyond the pain. So how can we face those putrefied, drippings wounds which have been exposed for some time? How should we react when we peer into our wounds? What should be our resolution on becoming aware that our wounds are exposed? These are some of the issues we struggle with profoundly.

"Have you tried counselling? I asked.

"Isn't that the same as seeing the psychologist and the social worker?" Sandra asked.

"What about a prayer session?" I suggested.

"My friends would love that!" Sandra interjected.

"I could organise it. We could probably have a half-night prayer session, sleep over and then have breakfast the next morning," I encouraged rather delightfully and eagerly.

"What do you mean? Will the prayer session heal the girls?" Sandra queried as she leaned forward in her chair, almost dropping to the floor in anticipation.

"Prayer is important. We never know what divine intervention can do," I responded.

We would agree that prayer is a vital spiritual activity for individuals who are seeking divine help. It is a discipline that helps the religious community to communicate with God. Although different religions have unique ways of engaging in prayer, the essential element of prayer is that it contribute to "the cultivation of a personal relationship with God, of a truly interior life, and of meditation on the basic truths of revealed religion."[15] In fact, a community who expresses its faith in the divine power often engages in caring acts such as prayer, visits and providing meals, thus demonstrating some degree of responsibility.

"I didn't know you could heal. Can you? Don't we need a vicar to conduct the prayer session?" she questioned in a searching manner.

I was caught 'between a rock and a hard place'. I sensed a pause. Will the determined parent-of-three be compliant and flexible and accept our suggestion even though I am not an ordained pastor? I pondered for a while. And then my thoughts ran away for a while. *Do I really have the gift of healing? Should I check out a pastor to lead the prayer session?* Although these were only thoughts, they are worth investigating.

From my research, I became aware that God clearly intended for us to be whole, peaceful and to live in perfect health. But how did God intend His initial desire for man's well-being to be perpetuated? Who should we carry our wounds to when we need healing? The Holy Scriptures aided me in discovering that God had revealed to the Jewish people that He is The Healer. Jesus also portrayed a similar thought by extensively engaging in a three-fold ministry, of which healing was a major part. We would agree that healing is essential for the building up of God's work on earth, until the return of Christ, the Saviour of mankind.

Nevertheless, Scripture contains numerous examples of God coming to the aid of human beings, by intervening "in the workings of nature" in which the "event that is so unusual... excites surprise and wonder." [16] Since healing and miracles are mentioned together in each of the three textual occurrences namely 1 Corinthians 12: 9, 28-30, the idea of miracles immediately suggests the occurrence of an event or phenomenon beyond human power. Certainly, divine healing is one such phenomenon. This assumption is based on the current definition which most modern dictionaries provide. An example of this is found in the third edition of *The Oxford Dictionary and Thesaurus* which defines a miracle as follows: "1: an extraordinary event attributed to some supernatural agency. 2a: any remarkable occurrence. 2b: a remarkable development in some specified area. Each of these linguistic entries refers to something beyond the ordinary and therefore, encompasses the general assumption as mentioned earlier.

Amazingly, at times, "the miraculous is meant the mysterious, the inexplicable"[17] indicating that the phenomenon would not be understood naturally. One instance of this is with Moses, the biblical character and Israel's leader in the book of Exodus. The biblical account informs us that he was startled by the non-consumed burning bush in the desert. God had appeared to Moses in the bush unexpectedly, yet the fire did not affect the bush, thus signalling a powerful, but incomprehensible event. When we consider healing in the context of miracles it "is probably due to the special ability of healing miracles to symbolize and communicate the saving power of God". [18]

Later that night, we had moved into Cynthia's dining room to be with Alex, Curtis and some of the others. This room was just as big as the living room, but more cluttered with household items. Dinner trays, table mats, and a tall mahogany cabinet for cutlery and china ware. A variety of fruits was resting in a flowered circular fruit bowl. Bright, juicy oranges. Smooth, jelly-like grapes. But Sandra seemed tensed. Something was on her mind.

"I wished this could be over. Stress and more stress! How comes I am hearing one thing from some people and something else from others? What's going on?" She demanded, throwing her hands in the air

"Let's have the prayer session," I assured her.

"O.K. I hope you are not leading me down a dead end," she warned.

Based on Sandra's sentiments, it would be useful to focus on the Holy Scriptures' perspectives on the gifts of healing: "There are different kinds of gifts, but the same Spirit. There are different kinds of service, but the same Lord. There are different kinds of working, but the same God works all of them in all men" (1 Corinthians 12:4-6, NIV). Here the Apostle Paul provides insights into the purpose of the spiritual gifts by linking the grace-gifts *charismaton* with ministries *diakonion* and workings *energematon*. There seems to be an inter-relationship among these three concepts, suggesting that spiritual gifts and in particular, the gifts of healing, should be used actively in serving God's people.[19] In reality, Christ bestows these gifts to his followers to prepare His people for service with the aim of establishing unity in the faith among believers. The Holy Scripture also provides the evidence: "Now to each one the manifestation of the Spirit is given for the common good. To one there is given through the Spirit the message of wisdom, to another the message of knowledge by means of the same Spirit, to another faith by the same Spirit, to another gifts of healing by that one Spirit" (1 Corinthians 12:7-9, NIV). Christ gives these gifts so that the recipients can use them to help build up the community

20

of Christian believers. In fact, the term 'common good' [*sumpheron*] is better understood in the Greek text which is translated 'to one's advantage' indicating that spiritual gifts, such as healing, benefits each believer. To do otherwise, we would be robbing God and His Church, and in turn, weakening His Kingdom.

"I still believe that we should have a prayer and bible study session," I added firmly.

"I agree," Alex replied.

Those in the room were stunned by all the turmoil. There was a hush. Nothing moved in the room. Not even the square-patterned curtains which covered the opened window moved! We could hear a pin drop! But it was short lived. Janice broke down in tears, and shouted,

"Mum, I am afraid."

She dashed out of the room in a flash, with painful tears dripping from her fear-infested eyes. Then she dropped to the floor, wailing and holding her head. Sandra, terrified by the turn of events, was trembling visibly as she dashed behind her emotionally distressed teenage daughter. She slumped to the floor trying to cuddle and comfort the weak girl.

Sandra's queries were understandable. In fact we should note that prior to Jesus leaving Earth, the selected Twelve Disciples had been accompanying Him on many trips. They had watched Him engaged in various aspects of ministry. Moreover, Jesus also equipped and empowered seventy other disciples to be involved in a healing ministry in the various communities. The chosen disciples were empowered to engage in ministry, so that they could obtain first-hand experience as they went out in groups of twos into the communities around them. These individuals were commissioned[20] to engage in a three-fold ministry: preach repentance, exorcise and heal by anointing. Such a group of ministerial activities was similar to those in which Jesus engaged while travelling through Jewish regions such as Galilee, Judea and Perea.

The Gospel of Mark presents the disciples as the first group of believers to be authorised to heal by anointing with oil, a commodity that was used as a medicine in the Greco-Roman world.[21] The sentence, in its active voice, and with an imperfect tense, 'they were anointing many sick people with oil' (St. Mark 6:13), indicates that they were engaging publicly in the ministry of healing. This was done continuously while they were still in the community among the people. With this perspective, the twelve disciples, who embarked on a specific mission as outline in the Second Gospel, displayed compassion like Jesus, for the suffering people.

In relation to this family's dilemma, we were taken aback by the latest development with Sandra and the girls. The situation moved us to heart-wrenching tears. We quickly huddled together and spent some time in prayer for Patricia, Janice, Judith and their mum. How do we respond when someone so close to us needs our assistance, but yet we are helpless? How do we help them face their open wounds? I had had enough. The prayer session was needed. We eventually settled for the half-night prayer service, two weeks later at 8 p.m. Janice's situation inspired us to agree on it. A few minutes after, Alex stretched. It was a sign that they were tired. We put on our coats, greeted each other good night and left.

When I revert to my research, I noticed that Jesus demonstrated his willingness to equip, empower and authorise His followers to engage in a healing ministry among other aspects of ministry. He emphatically assured the Twelve that those who believe in and accept Him will perform greater works than He has done. However, when we become involved in ministry, we are instruments in God's hands for reaching the hurting and the lost. Paul Avis reminds us that "All ministry is simply Christ at work through the presence of the Holy Spirit, leading, teaching and sanctifying his body through human – unworthy, and inadequate human – instruments."[22]

In light of the disciples being commissioned to engage in ministry, Jesus, just after his resurrection, reminded the disciples of their primary task, that of preaching the Gospel (St. Mark 16:15). Moreover, as they preached, Christ anticipated that others would believe on Him through the disciples' messages. With this being the case, Jesus outlined four signs that would accompany those who believe in Him, one of which is healing by the laying on of hands. This Christological pronouncement is advocated and expanded in James 5:13-16, where authority is assigned to a specific group of believers. Here, we observe that it is the leadership of the church, representing the whole church, who engages in the ministering to the sick.[23] From the textual evidence, it can be concluded that both the Twelve and subsequently, appointed church leaders had authority to engage in healing the sick. Ernest Lucas and Peter May even contend that "Since the Church is the agent of the Kingdom and continues Jesus' mission of preaching the gospel of the Kingdom, it is natural that it should include in this a healing ministry."[24]

It is evident also from the Holy Scripture that every Christian believer does not have the gift of healing. In fact, the Christian Church comprises of individuals who are all endowed with different spiritual gifts. Stephen Barton concludes that "each member of the fellowship is important and has a contribution to make" and as a result, "what each one offers is a revelation, not of human prowess, but of the power of the divine."[25] However, the Apostle Paul's rhetorical questions: Are all apostles? Are all prophets? Are all teachers? Are all workers of miracles? Do all have the gifts of healings? Do all speak with tongues? And Do all interpret (I Corinthians 12:29-30) substantiate the view that everyone does not possess all the spiritual gifts and certainly, not the gifts of healings.

A few days later, some of the young people met at Jane's parents' home. That evening, Cynthia, who was a mother-figure for many of these young people, had joined them. The intense discussion on the need to conduct the prayer session continued.

"I must be at that prayer session," shouted Yolanda, yet pensive.

"I will be there too," replied Curtis.

"So what will happen with the other half of the night?" shouted Yolanda, with her hands in the air.

"Yolanda, my dear, half night is from 8 p.m to midnight. We will sleep after that!" Cynthia reminded her.

"But wait though," Julian interrupted, "who is going to lead it?"

"Why did you ask?" Cynthia inquired.

"We could ask the trainee student to do it," Curtis suggested.

"I'm sure I heard people at church saying only trained leaders can have this sort of prayer session," Julian continued.

"If that's the case we should postpone this prayer thing," Sandra quickly stated.

"Is this how planning a prayer session is supposed to be?" shouted Janice, as she buried her head in a chair.

"Can't we check around to see if a pastor from one of the other churches can help?" suggested the vacillating mother-of-three.

"How do you know they can help us? You don't know what they believe," Julian interjected cautiously.

"I am sure they include healing in the services at some of these churches," Sandra reminded us.

"Janice or Patricia, can't one of you find out from the student pastor what some of these churches believe?" Julian requested kind-heartedly.

"And what's wrong with you? Can't you do it? Who do you think you are bossing me around?" Janice rebounded fiercely.

"You should do it yourself," Patricia replied astonishingly.

"Alright. Stop the arguing, the three of you! I will do it. It's our health at risk here," Sandra replied annoyingly.

Insightfully, my research revealed that, since Jesus commissioned the body of Christian believers to evangelise the whole world, it is fitting to conclude that the Church is expected to engage in the healing ministry which Jesus himself also conducted. In supporting the discussion surrounding the role of believers in divine healing, F. Martin indicates that healing and deliverance from demonic power are integral parts of evangelization [sic].[26] In particular, "those who are sent to preach the gospel," as Martin concludes, "are often endowed with the gift of healing as part of their empowerment to bring people to salvation.".[27] It is evident that selected leaders in the community of believers are entrusted with the authority to pray and conduct divine healing for the afflicted, who constantly face their wounds. Yet, while we face our own wounds, we become uncertain at times as to where we should turn. In spite of the perplexities that may confront us, we are assured that the God of Heaven can soothe our pain and uplift the discouraged heart.

**Thoughts for Action** *[Jot down your responses]*

- Are you able to handle your wounds at present/were you prepared to face your wounds in the past?

- How is your community responding to you? How did your community respond to you?

- How has this chapter helped you to face your wounds?

**Moments of Surrender**

- Is there a past experience with which you are in need of help? If writing it out would help, feel free to take you time and do just that here.

- Take some time to reach out to the God of Heaven by openly sharing the details with Him at this moment.

# 3

# The Views of a Few

*The New International Dictionary of Pentecostal and Charismatic Movements* reports that, since the year 2000, approximately 65.8 million people have been worshipping in 740 Pentecostal denominations in 225 countries worldwide. These 740 denominations are categorised, with some 660 being Classical Pentecostal denominations and the other 80 being Oneness Pentecostal denominations. The former sub-group are the traditional Western Pentecostals with some 63 millions worshippers globally. On the other hand, the latter are the Unitarian Pentecostals, who believe in and accept baptism in the name of Jesus only. On the other hand, there are approximately 175.8 million Charismatic Christian believers worshipping in about 235 countries. This multi-million member movement has about 6 530 denominations globally.[28]

Since 2008, there have been some 16.3 million baptised Seventh-day Adventist Christian believers worshipping in 128 390 congregations in 203 countries worldwide. If non-baptised worshippers and children are taken into account, the number rises to approximately 25 million.[29] Although these three movements are Protestants, from a theological standpoint, it would be exciting to delve into their beliefs and practices.

Resuming the interaction between Julian and Janice, he was taken aback. Janice was in tears. And tears began to brew in Patricia's eyes. Was Julian too harsh? Was he too critical? Was he robbing this ailing family of the ray of hope they desperately needed? Did he remind her about something at home?

"I was only checking, based on what I know," Julian remarked.

By this time Janice had recovered and was looking braver. But then, with her tear-stained face and completely bedraggled hair, she stood quietly near Judith, her younger sister, while mum leaned forward in her chair as if she was anticipating the unexpected. Soon after, Janice dropped slowly, but lifelessly, into the next nearby chair and soon fell asleep.

Whenever we are faced with the task of making a decision from among various options, anxiety, at times, sets in and clouds our thoughts. This family was eager to weigh its options. Desperation was evident from their desire to search elsewhere. It is possible that psychologically, mum was at breaking point and willing to take drastic action. Here, we come to grips with the hope-desperation tension that we often experience in our own lives. When we become overwhelmed with our demanding cares, discouragement set in at times and sadness speaks thunderously within our despondent hearts. During all of this we feel as though we are forgotten by our friends, our soul mate or even the God we pray to on numerous occasions. But it's the power of the Holy Spirit that sucks up our discouragement and replaces it with powerful hope in the God of the Universe. Although the battle may be raging ravenously within, a heart that is inspired by the Divine One finds jubilant joy in the thickness of our bleak situations.

While at home one Sunday afternoon, I was engrossed in a game as it rained profusely. The Easterly wind powerfully blew the rain onto the double-glaze windows. The transparent glass became translucent. Beyond the snow-like windows, I could barely recognise huge, thick, dark clouds hanging from the sky. Then my mobile phone rang.

"Hello!" I answered.

"Hi!" Sandra greeted me. "You are just the person I need," she announced.

"What's up?"

"I was doing some searching. What do you know about the Pentecostal churches?" she inquired forcibly.

"Well not a lot. Why?"

"Do you think one of their pastors can help the girls? What do you think?" she probed aggressively.

"I would have to check out their views and get back to you. Are you sure you about this?"

"See what you can find out. When we get to that bridge we will cross it," she interjected.

*Would she be prepared for the discoveries?* I wondered for a moment. On conducting the research, I became cognizant that healing is one of the many controversial issues in the religious world today. Such conflicts occur because various faith groups express their views differently on this crucial element of pastoral care. But healing also occupies "a prominent place in religious experience throughout the world" and when we address the issue of healing and sickness, "the meaning and value of ideas and experiences associated with healing become clear in the specific religious contexts in which they arise." [30] At the heart of Pentecostalism is the worship service where activities such as healings, exorcisms and praying aloud exist.[31] It is worth noting that apart from these activities, miracles are emphasized and these are what makes this religious movement "highly congenial to adherents of so-called primitive religions."[32] Within the Pentecostal movement, there is the general understanding that faith healing will form an integral part of the life of the congregations, thus providing deliverance from illnesses for its worshippers.[33] Notably, the vast number of Pentecostal believers upholds "Pentecostal theology or practice or stance, committed as denominations to Pentecostal distinctive."[34]

It is almost difficult to escape faith healing in the Pentecostal movement since the aims of religious healing are consonant with the overall goals of religious life in the culture of Pentecostalism. Sullivan also reminds us that "healing may be directed toward re-establishing ritual order, life in abundance, the expulsion of disorder and evil, redemption from condemnation, salvation from guilt and sin. In reality, "religious healing," he concludes, "clarifies the ways in which the individual human body lies at the center [sic] of sacred meaning."[35]

I return to Sandra's family and their debilitating emotional and physical issues. The time had arrived for me to gain some practical ministerial experience. Having being assigned the Tuesday evening bible discussion sessions, I prepared to conduct my first discussion class. Among the many eager and knowledge-hungry youth, were Patricia and Janice. During this session, Sandra remained behind with Judith, rather than travelling a long distance to return. As part of the programme, I allowed the youth to move into groups of fives and assign them a twenty-minute group activity. It was during this time that the searching mum approached me.

"Have you found out anything as yet?" she secretively asked.

"So far, Pentecostals believe strongly in faith healing and anointing. It's part of their worship. Give me some more time," I replied cautiously.

"I really need your help. Home and school have become very difficult, especially for Janice. I feel this is why she is not getting better," she shared, with her head leaned.

"What do you mean?" I asked.

"The social worker has insisted that Janice be sent to a foster home and my husband thinks the girls are faking their illnesses. Plus, he feels that I am not a fit mother. From the bottom of my heart, I have had enough. I don't think I can let this go on." she added.

Quickly after that, her mobile phone rang. She gingerly sauntered towards the door, while speaking to the caller. I was taken aback. I wondered how she would deal with Samuel's unsupportive and blaming attitude. Her goal was finding relief for the girls' ailing health at all cost. I pondered for a moment. Would she confront this hostile, unstable driver about his irresponsible behaviour and how his attitude is affecting the girls and her, emotionally? Having returned, she apologised,

"Sorry about that."

"Have both of you discussed the girls' situations?" I queried.

By this time there was excessive non-task talking in hall. It was a signal that the groups were ready for me.

"Let's talk later," I concluded quietly.

"Remember to continue checking that subject for me," she reminded me.

After allowing the different groups to share their thoughts on the different questions, I ended the session. Tiredness began to take over. We greeted each other good night and headed through the door.

Having resumed my research later over the weekend, it was evident from my digging, that the dynamism which is demonstrated among Pentecostal followers is due to the fact that they "invoke the power of the Holy Spirit, manifested through signs, wonders and charisms [sic], to aid in personal transformation, to break down the destructive, sinful structures in individual lives, and to bring relief from misery and death."[36] We can see from this focus the reason why "emphasis is placed on the role of the Holy Spirit to empower each person for some form of ministry"[37] hence, the reason the ministry of healing is carried out in these congregations. Apart from that they embrace the divine-healing doctrine and made it an aspect of their 'full gospel'. For the Pentecostals, the gospel is not restricted to the forgiveness of sins and the reconciliation of the "soul" to God, but extends also to the liberation and redemption of human society and the entire cosmos.[38]

In the later part of the next week, I stumbled upon Sandra as she waded through a human traffic in the city centre.

"Hi! How is it that you are in town at this time?" I inquired.

"Just browsing through town," she alerted me.

"Where are the girls?"

"They are at Cynthia's. They want to stay there for the evening and have a chat. Nothing much is happening at home, anyway. Apparently Alex and Curtis are joining them there also." she inserted.

"About the discussion we were having last Tuesday, I think you need to make your husband aware of what you all are going through."

"Every time I try to talk to him about our marriage, he trembles, becomes hysterical and walks away from me. He blatantly accuses me of not supporting him ever since we got married," she painfully shared.

"Take some time and write him a note letting him know how you feel and what you expect from him," I advised.

"Have you managed to get anywhere with what I was asking you about last time?"

"I should have something soon. Listen, I have to shoot off."

"O.K. Later."

When we take a careful study of the Pentecostal movement, it tends to focus greatly on being evangelical or proclaiming the good news of Christ. Yet the congregations are often centred on individual leaders within established churches.[39] Along with this feature, comes the emphasis on the need to cater to one's spiritual quests through various spiritual activities such as prayer and healing. I could not help but notice that such congregations within this movement encourage an emotional response to worship, while placing "emphasis on healing and human potential albeit in a spiritual guise."[40] Although Pentecostals and Charismatics share similar beliefs in the baptism of the Holy Spirit, the manifestation of the related gifts of the Spirit such as healing is more elaborate and revitalising. In particular, "Being filled with the Holy Spirit is an essential prerequisite for the capacity to praise,... and for the exercise of the spiritual gifts."[41] I gathered that Charismatics are very 'explosive' in their worship and seek to provide its members with an experience which sparks enthusiasm and life.

Turning back to Sandra's family difficulties, we had arrived at the church for our usual Tuesday evening bible studies. Most of the youth were late. This gave Sandra and I time to interact.

"Hi girls," I greeted.

Cynthia, her friend had come along and was offloading a box of snacks for the youth.

"Hi Sandra!"

"Hi. It looks as though many of the young people aren't planning to come," she replied jovially.

"Don't worry. They will turn up. How was your week?" I inquired.

"I did well in my assignments, but it was hectic at work with the clients. And then when I got home, being there didn't help."

"Do you think Samuel needs medication or maybe he is under pressure from the many cases he has?" I asked.

"Don't give me that. He attends clinic monthly. But he has been like this for as long as I can remember. And now he is hiding behind this mental problem. He's going to get the shock of his life soon," she responded assertively.

"But you know that those cases can be stressful. Especially when there is a backlog," I delved further.

"So should we suffer because of him? Is your head on right?"

Then she stared through the ceiling of the youth hall for a moment. How can we care for those who are desperately searching for a way out? It's the pleading heart of an individual that attracts his/her community with the hope that there will be a listening ear to hear the heart's anguish. A community that takes its responsibility seriously can accelerate one's relief, by pooling its resources together in a co-operative spirit. Would this industrious mother have this privilege?

"Don't do anything rash. You may regret it. By the way, I think it's best if I check out what your church believes in, concerning this healing business."

Soon after, the youth arrived. Unfortunately, they had planned to prepare for the worship service for the weekend. They wanted to spend the evening practising the songs and hymns. I surrendered the time to them. Within an hour, I was exhausted. I packed my bag and wished them good night.

Since I was studying theology, an entirely new subject area, for the first time, I felt the urge to check out the views of the Adventist Church on healing. A survey of Adventist publication indicates that this denomination takes a broader view of healing than the present usage. Various religious movements "confine healing largely to the physical," but "the holistic sense that pervades both the OT and NT requires that all aspects of the human experience are subject to healing, not the body alone."[42] Additionally, the bigger picture is considered in relation to Jesus' mission. Consequently, Adventists believe that Jesus' primary task was preaching the everlasting Gospel which produces "deliverance, forgiveness, reconciliation, rescue, and salvation, elements including but far surpassing physical relief."[43] Added to this is the view that "Physical healings held a place in a larger ministry" since Jesus "was first of all the Saviour, and physical healings were evidences, signs of His authority."[44]

Furthermore, while this denominational movement affirms the existence of gifts of the Spirit, spectacular and public display of these gifts are shunned by its followers. As a result, James 5:13-16 is used as the model for healing in its global congregations. The rule which adherents of Adventism and congregational leaders apply is seen in this text. The sick is expected to call the elders (and pastors), who will anoint them with oil and pray for their sickness in a specific way.[45] We can conclude that healing is not part of the worship service of this religious movement, but takes place when requested by ailing individuals.

Being intrigued by what I discovered, I telephoned Sandra the Sunday evening.

"Hello," she answered.

"Hi. I thought I would call to fill you in on what I have discovered. Basically, the Adventist's views on healing and those of the others churches I checked out are opposite in practice."

"What do you mean?" she pressed.

"Well, mainly the church practises private anointing and the person who is sick should request the anointing. The other churches tend to have it done publicly during their worship service. It seems to be 'on the spur of the moment'," I shared.

"Give me a few days. I need to think and pray about this one."

"Did I tell you that I left a message on my husband's mobile phone?"

"How did it go?"

"He didn't respond so I confronted him. He wasn't please. But I didn't care."

"What is happening now?"

"I told him something has to change. I will weigh my options carefully. In the meantime, I will wait around," she replied confidently.

While we look to God for help to attain healing for our wounds, we feel at times that we are on a waiting list. Yet, Jesus is still eager to extend relief to those whose bodies are inflicted with this world's barrage of diseases. When we are confronted with a sea of options, is it taxing, mentally, to choose correctly. Our hearts crave to move ahead, but we become stuck because we are waiting.

**Thoughts for Action** *[Jot down your responses]*

- To what extent did you have options to help you with your situation?

- How loyal are you to your community?

- Is there ever a time that you would turn away from your community, be it ethnic, church or professional?

- What would you do if you were confronted with conflicting options?

**Moments of Surrender**

- Do you feel confused and bewildered at this time? Take a moment to reflect on what you have read in this chapter.

- Is there anything that you can apply to your situation?

- What would you recommend to a friend who may be seeking relief from their wounds?

# 4

# On the Waiting List

In the months from June to November 2008, some 650 000 people were left homeless in Haiti as a result of hurricanes. Two hundred and fifty thousand were homeless in the Dominican Republic. Approximately 337 people died in four major Caribbean countries: Cuba, Dominican Republic, Haiti and Jamaica during the passing of Hurricanes Gustav, Hanna and Ike. Geologists believe that the earth's surface is becoming hotter, hence, there is a greater intensity of the hurricanes. Meteorologists focus on the changing of nature, with conditions such as pre-existing disturbance, warm ocean water, low atmospheric stability, moist mid-atmosphere, and upper atmosphere divergence all contributing to hurricane formation. Yet environmentalists blame human beings for polluting the atmosphere and affecting disaster-prone areas. Why is the world in such a mess if God is in control? How could the divine being who expresses love, let masses of people die from killer hurricanes, tsunamis, terrorist attacks and diseases? Why such bizarre carnage and chaos? Is the world coming to an end? Is He pouring out his wrath upon sinners? Why is it that we are greeted by the bloated bodies of the poor, the elderly, and the children strewn among the rubble? Questions like these force us to ponder on whether or not the God we hear about is all that powerful.

"Where is God when we need Him? Is He hearing my prayer? Why does it take so long before you can get help? It feels like eternity. Is God not interested in those who are hurting?" Sandra asked unreservedly.

These were some of the many expressed sentiments and questions that Sandra shared. Honestly speaking, we often conclude that we hardly see any signs of divine presence. We too look for something to give us hope in our moments of affliction. Importantly though, we are helped when we receive Christian pastoral care, the ministry that "is concerned with the well-being of communities or of individuals."[46] Such care can only be provided by the divine through lay or ordained pastoral care-givers who attempt to be in a harmonious relationship with Christ. The importance of the 'being' aspect of our relationship allows the Holy Spirit to give us *shalom* or inner peace, and in turn, provides us with God's power to encourage recipients of pastoral care to develop a similar relationship that could minimise human sufferings and struggles.[47]

Families like Sandra's can take comfort in the fact that the God of Heaven has empowered the Church so that His people can be cared for spiritually along with other areas of their lives. One way in which Christ manifests His care through the Church is in the ministry of healing.[48] We must understand that healing should be a central part of the life of the church because 'we all are wounded people' with spiritual, emotional, physical and psychological scars.[49] We experience agonising pain from these wounds and at times the consequences are harsh. We do not have to despair because Jesus, the Great Healer, is willing to restore our wholeness, even if not now, in the new earth. This acknowledgement of healing, however, is in relation to God's will, in that, not ever sick individual will be healed physically.

Nevertheless, it is sobering to know that "Since our relationship with God is fundamental to human well-being, [and] the spiritual and pastoral ministry of the churches, helping people to respond to the word of God, is a vital element in healing."[50] This would imply that sick individuals, even if they are not healed physically, can still experience emotional healing, an important phase that can help them cope with and continue their journey while in this present life. Besides, the suffering we experience can be best understood in terms of the 'wounded healer' to the point that we are more effective in healing the wounded when we have had "an experience of exposing our wounds to the forgiveness and healing" of the Holy Spirit.[51] By allowing the eyes of God to inspect our exposed wounds, this is an indication that we have moved beyond shame to experiencing comfort from His soothing touch.

The Holy Scripture reinforces this idea of comfort as seen in 2 Corinthians 1:3-4, where the writer of this biblical book noted that as The Divine One provides us with comfort, we can then support the wounded with what we have experienced personally. Interestingly, God our Creator is the Source of absolute encouragement, through whom afflicted individuals can experience emotional help and support during their difficult moments. In focusing on the repetitious use of the word *parakaleo* and its derivatives, in the text, we recognise the importance of this type of help. Here the idea of relief from affliction and a state of physical well-being emerges. This suggests that the re-assurance we receive is beyond the physical aspect, whereby someone is present to assist us in our distressing times. Moreover, in receiving such support, we can share from the depth of our own help and bring relief to those who are going through hard times. And certainly, even though sickness of any kind is seen as being tough, hard and distressing, it is not beyond the compassionate heart of God.

Why were Sandra and her children so desperate to get better? Was it God's will? Does God want her to live indefinitely with her hurts, pain and ailments? Questions like these move us to a new level in our spiritual relationship with God. Often times, it is our perspective of the situation that determines, to a large degree, how we respond. Some individuals are pushed away from God, resolving not to dabble with, believe in or trust in the Divine One. Such persons perceive Him to be powerless, uncaring and unreal. Individuals with this mindset, publicly express that God cannot be real because human beings experience great sufferings beyond measure. On the other hand, another individual is drawn closer to Christ, and sees Him as his/her Helper, Healer and Sustainer. For this individual, his faith and trust in God aids him/her in an understanding of God's grace. With these two views so popularly held, we would agree with Derek Tidball that before we intercede for the sick, "the mind of Christ needs to be discerned."[52]

When we reflect on the idea of waiting, we can think of the times we were on a waiting list for a house, a dentist, a special model car, a telephone line or even a place at a prestigious educational institution. We never expect to be turned down, lose, or be disappointed, much less fail. When we check on the progress of our application, we are told that we are on a waiting list. Emotions run high and questions flood our mind, which goes into overdrive. The thought of eternity flashes before us. The mere thought of waiting creates negative psychological reactions. We move into the fight-and-flight mode. Is there another way out? Another source? Shop? Institution? Housing agent? Or even car dealer?

These situations become more real. Often times we reach a point in our lives when we must wait. But then, at other times we are forced to wait. This family had been waiting for someone to bring relief for their inner wounds. No doubt, the theological motif of 'waiting' is prevalent in the psalmodic writings. The writer of Psalm 27 reminds us to "Wait on the Lord; be of good courage, and he shall strengthen thine heart: wait, I say, on the Lord" (v. 14, NKJV). Here the writer focuses repeatedly on the 'heart' (vv.3,8,13, 14), signalling its importance in addressing our emotional pain and sensing what we feel during those moments. By waiting on the divine presence, it aids us in listening to His voice and helps us put meaning to our experiences. As we progress through the Scripture, we discover that the 'waiting' motif also emerges in Psalms 25:5; 33:2 and many other psalmodic renditions.[53] The motif also has biblical references in both Old and New Testaments in the Holy Scriptures. This highlights our relationship with the God of Heaven, who was in the beginning (Genesis1.1; John 1.1), who is present in the form of the Holy Spirit (St. John 14:16-18) and who is coming in the form of Jesus, the Redeemer of the human race. Interestingly, waiting around can create opportunities to experience renewal and revival. Although waiting can be painful, nothing is lost, if we absorb the comforting moments that come our way.

In light of this perspective, let us ponder on four interconnected themes in this psalm: It is in Psalm 27:8 that we see the first theme, that of a willing heart. Waiting on God requires an individual to have a desire to be in His presence. We can therefore, express similar sentiments like the psalmist, asking the Lord to "Restore to me the joy of your salvation, and make me willing to obey you" (Psalm 51:12, NLT). But when trouble appears, whether in afflictions, sickness or trials, will we have the patience to wait for God to come to our rescue? In relation to these reflective questions, when we examine *levav,* the Hebrew word for heart, it denotes, apart from "emotions", ideas of "the mind" and "thoughts", thus indicating that the heart is the centre of human thought and spiritual life. Having this understanding, it signals the need for strong minds and fortified thoughts, a quality which the psalmist encourages us to acquire from the Divine One. Moreover, the prophet Isaiah provides additional comfort by reiterating that "those who wait on the Lord shall renew their strength; they shall mount up with wings as eagles, they shall run and not be weary, they shall walk and not faint" (40:31, NKJV). Certainly, a strong and willing heart is needed so that we may not be easily dissuaded from waiting on God to deliver us in our time of distress. Are we willing to wait on God, no matter how long He takes to respond to our pleas? It is the willing heart that goes after God passionately and such is what Christ desires us to have.

Secondly, the motive of the heart emerges, knowing that "The human heart is the most deceitful of all things, and desperately wicked. Who really knows how bad it is? But I, the LORD, search all hearts and examine secret motives. I give all people their due rewards, according to what their actions deserve" (Jeremiah 17:9-10, NLT). When we wait on God, what is our true motive: to receive blessings, a cure or to establish a closer relationship with Him? What thoughts pass through our minds? Can they stand up to the divine scrutiny? It is critical to our waiting on God, because "man looks at the outward appearance, but the Lord looks at the heart" (1 Samuel 16:7, NKJV).

According to Willem S. Prinsloo, Psalm 27 is an individual lament, which "is not simply a description of suffering; its purpose is rather to obtain an end to the suffering and to move closer to God."[54] In light of emotional distress and physical ailments, since the heart feels the emotional pain, we can identify with and incorporate psalms of lament in our quest for divine intervention, knowing that they can express the true sentiments of our innermost being. However, when we reflect on the impact of life's struggles on our spiritual development, we realise the "Psalms of 'lament' acknowledge that life does not consist of prosperity only, but that it also has pain, grief, darkness, and evil."[55] Focusing on the third theme, that of expressing our inner pain, we see from this perspective, that we have a context through which we can express, from the heart, our deepest needs, especially when we are afflicted with an ailment or are experiencing severe difficulties.

The fourth theme appears in the two dimensions portrayed in the form of petitioner-enemy-God which is evident in many psalms. Importantly, 'Lament' psalms, such as Psalm 27, seek to persuade on two levels, where petitioners calls on God, urging Him to alter the divine attitude towards them.[56] As the psalmist waits on God, he perceives God as 'my light', 'my salvation', and 'strength of my life'. These terms bring hope to petitioners like us, whose confidence must rest in the powerful God. Additionally, on the other level, psalms of 'lament' persuade the petitioner to trust wholeheartedly in God, despite prevailing pressure from our enemies. As we seek to experience healing for our ailments and at the same time, grow spiritually, we find ourselves caught up in "a dynamic triangular relationship" where interaction between the agents is intense, fierce and supernatural.[57]

Emerging from this is the simple point that we cannot experience healing without pleading to God to respond to His various promises. Neither can we accomplish such a blessing without counteracting and resisting the evil forces through fervent, earnest prayer. In our spiritual walk, we cannot reach out to God without being hindered vehemently by the enemy of our souls, since he has "not come except to steal, and to kill and to destroy" (John 10:10, NKJV). Moreover, we cannot wrestle passionately with evil forces without tapping into the supernatural power of the Almighty and all-powerful God. So, while we crave earnestly for healing, we must be cognisant of the fact that waiting on God implies watching for the adversary.

On a South Korean beach in Busan, almost a year ago, a brave American Second Infantry Division Soldier gave the gift of life to a 9-year-old Korean girl. On that almost fateful summer day when the warm water of the East Sea (Sea of Japan), flowing westward out of the Pacific Ocean, lapped against the rocks and sand of the Haeundae Beach, this brave soldier was swimming a little way from the shore with another colleague. The Korean beautiful 12-kilometre coast line, with its white sand, green pine trees and hot spring, is home to an affluent and attractive beach front community that lures tens of thousands of Korean tourists and foreigners to the beautiful site that many consider to be Korea's best beach. While enjoying himself in the most popular beach in Busan, South Korea's second largest metropolis, the fast-acting military personnel suddenly heard loud frantic screams from sun-soaked people on the beach pointing to a place beyond the waves, more than 50 yards out into the water. Inspite of busy activities on Haeundae Beach, where several kinds of beach festivals normal take place, the sharp shouts burst through the noise and attracted the soldier. In the distance, a frail frightened and fear-stricken little girl was struggling for her life as she tried desperately to keep her head above the Japanese water.

Meanwhile, another girl, standing waist-deep in the choppy water between the waves, was crying for help. As the courageous soldier assessed the situation, he noted that the fierce waves were swelling up and the little girl was caught between them in deep water. As the boisterous Pacific water was about to swallow its victims, the two girls yelled even louder, hoping that somebody would rescue them since they were in trouble. Instantly, the American swam quickly to the girls, wrapped his arm around their shoulders and swam back through the waves toward the shore where his colleague stood by to help bring them ashore. Several people entered the water to help take the shaken girls to shore, having been saved from drowning.

Similarly, I could not help but think that Sandra and her girls have been screaming internally for help because they were in trouble. More seriously, they were about to drown with severe illnesses and emotional difficulties. Couldn't anyone hear their cries like the brave soldier? Did anyone see the struggles that they faced daily? Reverting to Sandra and her family, as the days rushed by, Patricia struggled painfully to get a proper sleep at night. There were very few mornings that she made it anywhere on time because of the sleepless nights. The tiredness was eating away her precious energy. Deep frustration was etched visibly on her pain-soaked face. Although the outwards signs indicated a search for relief, I could almost sense a resignation in this family to just move along with the tide of their difficulties. The questions continued to emerge from the lips of the suffering children, along with their mum.

"What are you going to do about Janice? Is there nobody who can at least do something for us?" Patricia asked longingly.

"We are still looking forward to the prayer session. Have a little patience," Sandra explained encouragingly.

"I don't want to go on like this," Patricia demanded.

Mum's heart continue to beat in anticipation, yet fearful that there will be no help for her hurting children, let alone herself. This family's painful ordeal reminds me of a biblical story in the Gospel of Mark, where a father brought his sick son to Jesus' disciples so that they could heal him. The father's heart must have been pulsating immensely as he searched for support for his sick son. How long was the boy suffering with this issue? Was the father looking for help before coming to Jesus or was this illness a sudden occurrence? Scripture is silent on these issues. Nevertheless, there was a family in need of a healing touch that would relieve the boy who was being thrown to the ground frequently. He often foamed at his mouth and his teeth clattered against each other and he became stiff. What a heart-wrenching sight for a parent to witness! No doubt the father had to provide round-the-clock care for the boy, thus, he saw every attack that he suffered. The father's anticipation heightened because he believed that since Jesus, the Master, was unavailable, at least his disciples could bring relief to his ailing son.

However, on approaching the disciples, dad experienced shock and cold amazement on learning that the disciples lacked the healing power to restore wholeness to the boy. Although they travelled with Jesus on numerous ministry trips, where they witnessed and experienced the power of God, the disciples themselves were not power rangers. The searching father's pumped-up balloon of anticipation had burst. Pop! His world was about to collapse. The long desired hope was about to fade into thin air. What do we do when we search for help, support and an opportunity for encouragement, but discover that it is absent? How do we address our disappointments, particularly in our time of physical and emotional pain? How to you respond when your community fails you?

Dad and his son had to endure greater pain as they waited for Jesus to turn up. Did the disciples line up in front of the sick boy? Did they identify a few of the disciples to heal him? The biblical account does not address these issues. Yet, in whatever way they attempted to help the suffering child, he was on the waiting list. How do we feel when we are on God's waiting list? How do we respond when we are put on hold? How long does God put us on His waiting list? What should we do while we wait? Is God's response dependent on who is in front of us? Certainly, the order of our case does not impact on God's power to respond to us. Importantly, He sees our tears when they stream down our sullen cheeks and He hears our desperate pleas.

Returning to the journey of Sandra, Patricia, Janice and Judith, the time for the prayer session had arrived. Having attended at least one church service for the day, tiredness took its toll on our bodies. But this family of four needed our prayers. At the end of the inspiring church services, we made our way to Cynthia's home. About six eager young people and five adults soaked up every available space in the Cynthia's living room that windy Saturday night. Many of them carried faces of sheer anticipation. The atmosphere was unusual. One by one, everyone found a chair, positioned it in any available space and sat with locked fingers, waiting for the next move. After a short prayer and greetings, Cynthia took out the Olive oil, fetched a saucer from the cabinet and placed them in the middle of the room. I briefly explained the procedure, and then we selected favourite hymns and songs. As the young people sang fervently, inspiringly, but softly, beams of hope lit up their faces. At times Patricia had to hold her ears. Janice was smiling broadly, thus indicating some sense of relief. After the third song, Norman, a family friend of Cynthia's, quietly walked into the room. The time had come for us to pray. I knelt down, took the bottle of Olive oil and poured some into a saucer.

"Bang!" There was a loud crash outside.

"Did anyone hear that?" Cynthia asked.

The thick black darkness of the night began to force its way into the packed room. Along with it came a whistling breeze. Cynthia, looking up, saw her pink floral curtains blowing against the nocturnal breeze. For a moment, fear gripped our hearts. No one moved. Then Norman went to check that everything outside was intact. Meanwhile, Yolanda, afraid of the darkness, huddled behind her friend, Alex. The whistling noise struck fear into some of our hearts.

"Norman hasn't come back as yet. Why is he taking so long?" Curtis queried.

"Julian, check what's happening outside with Norman," Mrs. Bruce, his mother, advised.

It felt like eternity before Norman could return. Soon after Julian had left, both of them quickly returned, not displaying any signs that there was a problem. Mrs. Bruce, the fifty-five-year-old mother-of-four, produced a motherly smile, on seeing that both young men had returned safely. The active, but restless matriarch looked over at Cynthia. The optimistic nurse, of middle size and strongly built, gave us an assurance:

"It looks O.K now. We won't have any more disturbances."

Then we resettled and regained our focus. We softly hummed a hymn to regain our spiritual focus.

"Let's only have the prayer," cautioned Mrs Bruce.

"Does everybody feel the same way?" I inquired.

"Yes," they all replied in chorus.

I felt confused. But I succumbed to the voices around me. Soon after, we regrouped and formed a circle. Everyone bowed, as if in anticipation that everything will go well that night. Such reactions echoed the sentiments expressed by Francis Martin, that "healing individuals of spiritual, emotional or physical ailments sets in motion a process of reconciliation, restoration and liberation which are gained from the power of the cross through the preaching of the Gospel." [58] We listened to the voices, but I was still uncertain about the new request. Afterwards, we greeted each other good-bye and then rushed off briskly since it was late into the night.

I am reminded of an intriguing story taking place near the rocky landscape of the Jewish pool called Bethesda in the busy metropolis city of ancient Jerusalem, where Jesus traversed. Having manoeuvred through the streets, with the white undulating Judean mountains surrounding Him, Jesus approached five stone sheds or porches. They were all filled with a sea of infirmed and helpless people. The physical disabled, the hearing impaired, the paraplegic, quadriplegic those with a speech impediment and the paralysed were all present. Were they born that way? Did they stay there at the pool all day long? Did some of them turn up in the morning only? The Holy Scriptural account provides no insights on these issues. Nevertheless, this must have been a pitiful sight since most of these individuals had no human help or support. It was a case of each person for him/herself.

The writer of the biblical book of John's Gospel informs us that these individuals were waiting for the water to be stirred. Indeed, the waiting period was unpredictable because the sick individuals had to wait on an angel, who appeared unannounced and intermittently, to stir the water. In fact, everyone became aware of the angel's presence. Such heavenly messengers appear with a radiant and glorious light that beamed hope into the people's lives. Perhaps these individuals kept their eyes on the clear azure sky and prayed fervently that it would not rain. It is possible that the rustling of the tree leaves, the flapping of the birds' wings or even the howling of the breeze, travelling over from the mountains adjacent to the dead sea, may have awaken their passion to reach the pool. It was very likely that the strong ones inched their way near the edge of the special pool. Some may have crept, others may have hopped and a few may have dragged themselves, inch by inch, to be parked near the pool's edge.

Truthfully, there was a fiery passion in these sick individuals to approach the coveted pool because the first person to enter was healed of whatever disease or ailment he/she had. They must have been waiting for what felt like eternity because Jesus stumbled upon a gentleman, who was sick for thirty-eight years. Was he at the pool for 38 years? Was he 38 years old? Or was he just sick for 38 years? Jesus' eyes zoomed in on him and immediately His heart went out to him. Actually, John, the writer, informs us that Jesus, who is all-knowing, was aware that the man was living like that for a long time. It was then that Jesus inquired about his desire to be healed.

Being pre-occupied with a lack of able-bodied human support, he reminded Jesus of his weakness and his inability to reach the pool before many of the other more determined sick individuals moved ahead of him. In fact, he painfully reminded Jesus of the great effort that he made daily to enter the long-sought after water. That must have been heartbreaking! He must have been disappointed on numerous occasions. Perhaps, whenever he crept along the dusty and rocky terrain, he felt a hot human breeze rushing past his body. Nevertheless, Jesus provides new hope for him. He instructed the disadvantaged man to stand up, remove his bed and move out from among the sick people. What a relief after being on the waiting list for so long! We feel this way at times. We wonder when will out healing moment come. We look eagerly for that occasion when Christ will show up and bring a breeze of hope into our lives. More often than not, it is not about when will our moment appear, but whether or not we have the patience to stay on the waiting list.

Sometime during the next few weeks, some of Sandra's friends met at Cynthia's for a night of fun and games. It was very probable that the noise would be too much for Patricia, so she occupied the spare bedroom upstairs, trying to make up for the many sleepless nights. As we walked on the dark green neatly laid carpet, it screamed in agony. The sturdy sofas seem to cry out from the battering they took during previous games nights. Although the plain double-glazed windows were positioned equally around the late-twentieth Century building, we could hardly take in the view at the back because of the blackness of the night.

"I heard that you are doing special bible studies," announced Julian, in a good-humoured manner, looking at Janice.

"How did you know?" Janice demanded.

"And what is it to you?" pushed Patricia.

"Are you planning to get baptised or something?" Julian asked inquiringly.

"What's wrong with studying the bible? Janice blurted out, looking directly into Julian's eyes.

*Would she pounce on him? Would she attack Him? Would she fold in with tears?*

When we reflect on families like Sandra's, we cannot help but ask that searching question: What can families who are riddled with inner pain expect from a time of prayer? By engaging in this religious discipline, the spiritual dimension of our lives is ministered to, thus bringing some degree of peace to our minds. While we search frantically for holistic restoration, we must remember that "Healing is part of the atonement that Jesus accomplished through his death and resurrection, that's why the biblical prophet, Isaiah, could have exclaimed that by his stripes we are healed, while the writer of the Epistle of Peter echoed the same sentiments."[59]

In agreeing with such views, Francis Martin advocates that "the primary purpose of healing is to demonstrate tangibly God's intention and ability to lead people to the ultimate salvation, which is eternal life – i.e, the fruit of healing is conversion."[60] Yet, even though "physical healing does more than rectify disorders of the body" when we truly reflect on the impact of prayer, fasting and even studying the Holy Scriptures, we would agree that when these spiritual disciplines are blended with a time of healing, "it makes God present to the one healed."[61]

**Thoughts for Action** *[Jot down your responses]*

- In what way(s) can you identify with this family?

- What has your waiting experience been like?

- What care or comfort have you experienced while waiting?

- To what extent was the waiting period beneficial for you?

- How is your community responding to you/ How did your community respond to you?

- How has this chapter helped you to face your wounds?


**Moments of Surrender**

- Is there a past experience with which you are in need of help? If writing it out would help, feel free to take you time and do just that here.


- Take some time to reach out to the God of Heaven by openly sharing the details with Him at this moment.

# 5

# In the Good Old Days

A nomadic group of frightened people was on the run from the violent and brutal mistreatment of the regal leader of an ancient country. Hours before their nocturnal departure, the members of this nomadic multitude most probably showed a good face to their neighbours. They smiled with them. They carried out whatever task they wanted. Perhaps they even volunteered to do extra work, free of cost, for these neighbours. The neighbours' hearts melted towards the destitute and scattered people. In the end, they craftily seized valuable possessions of all kind: shining silver ware, glittering golden utensils, comfortable clean clothes, and even specially selected sheep.

However, the night had brought regrettable grief and horrific sorrow. It was awful. Mothers wailed pathetically because members of this ancient country lost their firstborn sons to death. Fathers wept in sorrow. Children screamed in anguish. Even the animals groaned as they witnessed their young dropping to the ground, lying as stiff as board. It was a dark night in the palace when the inevitable news reached Pharaoh, the biblical character, that the relieved multitude of people was filing out of his beloved city. His heart immediately swelled with anger and his face was like crimson as he was incensed with rage. It would appear that the process of osmosis had occurred because the king's loyal servants also became enraged. Their hearts breathed feelings of hatred towards these nomadic helpless people. Immediately there was confusion. Uncertainty. Inner turmoil. Perplexity. The Commander-in-chief, turning to his second-in-command, posed the unexpected question:

"Why have we released those people?"

No one could give a sensible and sound political reason for releasing the enslaved nomads. Shouts must have riveted the special meeting room. Perhaps the king paced to and fro and pulled his long brown hair, looking for an effective solution. Perhaps he peered into the eyes of the standing officers, as if to say 'you should have seen this coming'. Each of the well-groomed and stylishly-dressed trusted officers remained sealed to his spot- in military position-with their weapons neatly gripped in fear. Not a fly dared flap its wings at this moment. Then, without hesitation, the silence broke. The king, being the Commander-in-chief, ordered six hundred of the best soldiers to prepare for combat. The mission - to hunt down the fleeing nomadic group. Instantly, the glittering metallic gong, positioned over the guard wall, spoke authoritative. Since every military force, including platoon commanders, charioteers, infantry men and the navy, was expected to be ready at a moment's notice, the specially selected armed forces and horse-drawn chariots with mounted soldiers appeared in the palace courtyard in a flash. While waiting, the horses seemed to have been charged for their assignment, as they chewed ferociously on the iron reins. Simultaneously, they trotted impatiently, as if they wanted to get on with the 'job at hand'.

Meanwhile, as a brave military commander, the king notified his second-in-command to prepare his special chariot without delay and be in position to lead the troops. As soon as the king mounted his chariot, he signalled to his driver. While the mighty chariots were thundering through the streets, the liberated nomads were marching boldly and triumphantly towards their escape point. Laden with their precious possessions, they traversed the terrain firmly and upright. Their heads were held high. Eyes looking ahead. Hands occupied to the maximum. Somewhere in the middle of the uniformed procession, a family of four jokingly mocked the soldier at the palace's gate.

"Did you see how the poor guard was spinning around like a peacock, when I was waving at him from the wall?" the eldest son remarked.

"Oh, that was funny. He didn't even have a clue of what we were up to," Dad added.

"Well, he must have lost his brain. He didn't even see this large golden jar that I sneaked out."

By now, mum had had enough: "Come on, this is no time for joking around. This is a serious long journey."

But back in the roaring chariots, with hatred pulsating from his cruel heart, the king increased the speed of his chariot. With real horse-power, the charged soldiers caught up with the pedestrians. By this time the nomadic group was camping by the seaside. Their weary and blistered feet needed rest. The cluttered hands and head needed time out. The dehydrated animals needed a drink of the cool refreshing water. But while the nomadic group was concentrating on being refreshed, a shocking sight confronted them.

Far off in the distance, a sheet of darkness had already spread over the atmosphere. Emerging out of this darkness, some of the nomads heard the wheels of the chariots rattling boisterously along the rugged road. A few people were alerted to the high pitch noise and lifted their heads above the horizon of heads. Then the rattling noise grew louder and louder, as the army came closer and closer. Immediately, fear paralysed everyone. Fear of being re-enslaved. Fear of losing their only earthly possessions. Fear of losing their liberty. Fear transformed a group of bold, decisive and focused people into a sea of crying victims. Fear can be crippling, especially when it conceals the future from our eyes. It affects the mind, thus preventing individuals from thinking logically and strategically. Moreover, it blinds us to our possibilities. This emotive feeling prevents us from moving forward. Unless we overcome our fear of people, fear of our environment and fear of inabilities, we are unable to be effective in assisting each other in areas of concern.

Suddenly, an outspoken liberal nomadic leader sparked and exploded:

"Did you bring us out here by the seaside to bury us because there were no graves in the King's city?"

The nomadic top leader was deeply in thought.

"The good old days would have been better. We missed serving King Pharaoh!" this liberal leader continued spouting.

*Would the top leader shoot him down for insubordination? Would he ask some of the bodyguards to silence him?* The top leader was conspicuously absent.

"This dark, barren, hopeless wilderness is not for us. It cannot match with the King's cities."

By this time, the top leader stood up and held out his rod. Immediately, a miraculous sight lifted everyone to his/her feet. They saw the sea splitting into two and moving towards the sky making two separate walls in the night. Without hesitation, the top leader ordered his people to step out onto the dry land. But by this time, King Pharaoh was approaching the edge of the sea. By the time the nomads had stepped onto the dry land on the other side of the sea, the wall began descending. There were screams. Screams from the soldiers. Screams from the horses. Screams from the boisterous sea waves, as they hungrily swallowed their victims. Exhausted. Weary. Afraid. Trembling. The nomads sat down to recuperate from their near-death experience.

Later, as they recovered, their stomachs began growling with hunger. Certainly, there were no shops or bakeries in the wilderness.

"Where is the food?" someone queried.

They felt that starvation would dig graves for them in the wilderness. And their minds rolled back to the good old days they had with King Pharaoh.

"It would have been better if Pharaoh and his soldiers had killed us."

"Can we not get some of that tasty baked meat or mouth-watering bread which we had back in the King's house?"

Similarly, we hunger for the good old days we lived through long ago. The former community spirit. Culture. Music. And cosy conversations with neighbours. At time we wonder if we will ever return to those days. What makes us crave for the good old days? Nostalgia? Compensation for what we did not get the chance to accomplish? The good old days had their advantages and incomparable merits. But unless we are willing to push ahead with our present lives, we can become stuck in holding on to 'the good old days'.

In fact, psychologists have noted that nostalgia has therapeutic advantages. Nostalgic episodes promote psychological health. In particular, individuals, who revert to thoughts of special people who are close to them or significant events and places in their lives, experience high self-esteem and have a greater sense of being loved. While loneliness can trigger nostalgia, it is the nostalgic thoughts that can counteract a sense of loneliness.

Turning back to Janice's short encounter with Julian, she put her hand in the air, showed him the palm of her hand and turned away contemptuously, as if he did not exist. Quickly after, she made a bee-line into the far right-hand corner, where Jim was setting up the CD player to provide much needed quiet music. The excited teenagers and the energetic youth were eager to get the fun and games started. No doubt he would be playing quiet gospel stuff from singing sisters, Mary, Mary and some of Kirk Franklin's lively music, along with other varieties. At the same time, Cynthia, along with Curtis and Sophia, were hurriedly putting out the delicacies: crisps, popcorn, cheese sandwiches and potato chips. While being busy, Curtis kept his eyes on Julian, who was leading the games as he tried to finish the preparation. It was as if he was saying 'I don't want to miss those games. Wait, don't end it yet, I am coming.' As Sophia glanced up, her eyes made four with Janice's. At that moment, the 'fun and games' session in the middle of the room had become more animated and highly competitive. Some of the youth, however, trickled over to the food table to grab some of the goodies to replace expended energies.

Later, a few individuals hurriedly waved their hands, and began rushing to the door. When I glanced at the small metal-rim Quartz clock on the wall, it was making twelve midnight. Cynthia immediately signalled to everyone that it was time to pack up. We helped to tidy the living room and then headed for the door. Meanwhile, Sophia checked to ensure that everyone had transportation to his/her home. We waved good night and each of us went his/her way.

The following Tuesday night, Patricia, Janice and I arrived at church for our bible studies session. Meanwhile, the church's song leader had arrived with her team to prepare for the weekend's church service. After setting out the material, I was about to sit in a horseshoe teaching style, when Sandra passed a note to me. There was a tight grin on her face. In the note she requested to speak with me urgently after the study session. At times, the music was overbearing for Patricia. We had to ask the leader to reduce the volume. By 8:30 p.m, the studies had come to a close. We packed away the materials and headed for the door. There Sandra sat with Judith, seemingly engrossed in her own affairs, but taking in the melodious music. On our way to the car park, she sent the children to her car, while she and I stood by mine.

As she shared her concerns with me, she was gesticulating frequently with her hands, while shaking her head.

"I have had enough of this home situation. I am not going to put up with Samuel's pretence that he is ill. That's it." She declared.

Feeling a bit uncomfortable with taking on this issue, I inquired:

"What are you thinking about doing?"

"I was planning to see my solicitor to get some advice about this situation."

"Don't you think a counsellor or a therapist could help?

"What are you suggesting? I want to move on with my life. I can't keep going on like this," she replied, shaking her head determinedly.

"Is there any place you can get away for a break- to get some time to think things over? This might be better, because it may give him time to think also," I counselled.

"That may not work because I have to work. And the girls would have to come also. But also if I move out he may want to use that against me, because that is what he would want," the patient democratic-style parent shared with me.

I sensed the need to remind her of some of the consequences she will have to face.

"Remember, there are lots of important issues you have to consider-the girls, housing and finances. Can you afford to cope with all of these demands?

"Well I am not planning to move out because I have put all of my money into that house over the last four years. There is no way I am going to leave. Anybody leaving, it would have to be him. He hardly helps financially, even though he works for more money than me," this good-natured, but easily swayed wife declared assertively and confidently.

In times like these, our faithfulness becomes critical to our connection with the God of Heaven. It's a sign that He is first in our life. *Why did this desperate emotionally tired mum not refer explicitly to God in her conversation with me as she 'grasped' for help?* I thought. It seems evident that while involving God in this issue was critical, despite her strong spiritual faith, she seemed to lack the inner spiritual 'drive' at the time to initiate contact with God. Perhaps she may not have felt as close to him as she would have liked to be.

I became worried. Will this modest support worker force her unstable husband out of the matrimonial home so that she and her ailing children can be emotionally stable? There was a pregnant pause. At that moment, it felt like eternity. She smiled. I noticed a thought or two swimming around in her mind. *Was she contemplating on her next move? Was she expecting her self-conscious husband to vacate the house without any fuss? Was she thinking about the future when she and the girls would have some tranquility?* I thought.

"What's the matter?" I queried.

"I was just thinking about the good times we had during the early days of our marriage, especially when we were overseas. I wish things could still be that way. Then she admitted:

"I'm sure there is a way out. If God could help people in the Old Testament times, can't he help me today?" she asked longingly

"Remember, God still cares about your struggles just as He did for the people in the bible," I assured her firmly.

Her question was the clue for me to re-embark on more research. In order to have my facts in place, I had to investigate this critical issue, that of the Old Testament perspective of healing. From a survey of the Holy Scriptures, we see a direct relationship between God and the people of Ancient Israel- healer-patient. Jehovah declares His ability to heal in the biblical book of Exodus. The Scriptures relate the following divine pronouncement: "If you listen carefully to the voice of the LORD your God and do what is right in his eyes, if you pay attention to his commands and keep all his decrees, I will not bring on you any of the diseases I brought on the Egyptians, for I am the LORD, who heals you. Worship the LORD your God, and his blessing will be on your food and water. I will take away sickness from among you" (23:25, NIV).

Other evidence of this healer-patient relationship exists in other parts of the Pentateuch, namely in the book of Numbers. The people of Ancient Israel, on becoming impatient, discouraged and disrespectful, defied God's leadership and challenged Moses, their leader. Scripture puts it bluntly: "They began to speak against God and Moses. 'Why have you brought us out of Egypt to die here in the wilderness?' they complained. 'There is nothing to eat here and nothing to drink. And we hate this horrible manna!' (Numbers 21:5, NLT). In response to this humane and emotional outburst, God allowed venomous snakes to invade the people's tents, resulting in many deaths. Being remorseful, the suffering people pleaded with Moses that he should pray for them. In response, God instructed Moses to produce the antidote in the form of a bronze replica of the biting snakes. The healing occurred when the people, in faith, focused on this symbol of God's Banner. By lifting up the bronze serpent, Moses was echoing similar expressions in Exodus 17:15-16, where he "built an altar and called it The LORD is my Banner. He said, 'For hands were lifted up to the throne of the Lord,'" (NIV). Interestingly, this 'dissatisfaction story' demonstrates the compassionate heart of the God of Heaven who showed mercy to a multitude that was destined to be annihilated. Nevertheless, even though the people requested the healing, it took place on a mass scale in a public context. This demonstrates that God is not restricted by the private or public sphere to alleviate our pain.

What resources do we draw on to aid the sick, the suffering, and the weak? When we care for the vulnerable and the disadvantaged, we display personal and community responsibility. Our caring attitude speaks volumes. Such actions reach the core of their trembling hearts and bring comfort and peace of mind. Life has harsh journeys. But the pains and anguish endured on the paths of such journeys can be soothed with spiritual resources such as prayer and counselling. In fact, Jehovah's omnipotence is often displayed in the mundane and simple events in life. While we desperately desire relief in times of difficulties, we must be aware that God is unpredictable, hence coming to our rescue in unorthodox ways.

On returning to the conversation with this trusting, but hot-tempered mother, I inquired,

"Are you getting any financial help with your studies?"

"Well, the good thing is the government pays my fees and gives me a monthly grant."

"It would be good if you could make it stretch," I added advisedly.

"But there are still other bills to be paid and the home to maintain. I can't go on killing myself and my husband living freely."

I paused for a while. This appeared to be marital suicide. Her various coping strategies seemed to be ineffective. I needed to time to think through this one. I felt this was too much for me. I felt lost for answers. I didn't have the resources. Then a light flashed in my mind.

This family's ordeal is one where mum takes responsibility for her infirmed children. But the opposite occurs often in our world. Sometime after the exciting Football World Cup 2010 in South Africa, a number of courageous researchers set out to investigate an African reality that will linger long after the festive occasion of the World Cup. A number of British and South African researchers inquisitively engaged in a phenomenal research by questioning more than 7,000 people in some of South Africa's poorest townships. They set out to investigate the state of the mental health and level of education of those South African children who had become carers for their relatives with HIV and AIDS. **Many of these potentially-bright children had become life-long orphans** due to the bitter ravages of the deadly AIDS disease. The researchers discovered that these bereft children suffered higher levels of psychological distress than orphans whose parents had died of other causes. These despondent urban children are more likely to contract HIV themselves.

Apart from the high probability of experiencing psychological problems, they also wore a stigma 'sign'. Many of their friends avoided them, gossiped about them and teased them. Worst yet, people have been scared to touch them. They experienced bullying in their districts. And there is hardly any social support or access to appropriate medicine for their ailing loved ones. The reliable kids have been elated to share the secret debilitating illness in their financially-strapped family. What's even more difficult is the deplorable circumstances in which they subsist. If there are not riots in Cape Town, there are gangsters in Durban, and outbreaks causing health risks in Mpumalanga. Open sewers are on some streets. And long-overdue rubbish heaps, waiting to be cleared, give off a pungent stench. Being carers of AIDS-sufferers, many of these African children have had to miss or drop out of school. These horrific experiences demand urgent help since it is hard to come face-to-face with families whose lives are destroyed beyond repair. [62]

Although Sandra, along with help from Cynthia, tirelessly cared daily for her treasured daughters, they reliably supported each other, whether it was washing dishes, vacuuming the carpet or putting the washing on the line to dry. Caring for each other was reciprocal. Continuing the conversation with Sandra in the car park, as the bright, radiant light beamed in my mind, I inserted:

"I always say to people that they need to give the Lord something to work with. You need to involve Him in this matter. If you go to the bureau, it looks as though God can't help you."

"I understand that, but I am just going to get some information," she pushed.

"This is what I can do for you. Let's spend a week in prayer and fasting. After that you can make your move. That is the best thing I can think of now," I added, with internal trembling.

At such times, we must be able to perceive that there is a divine solution to our 'octopus' problems and therefore, give God room to intervene freely. The suggestions to involve God in this family's prevailing crisis and to pray and fast echoed Proverbs 3.6: "In all our ways acknowledge Him and He shall direct our path." It is through this reflection that I pictured a caring and compassionate God, who being touched by Sandra's emotionally-destroying situation, was willing to respond to her request. This seemed to have provided a ray of hope for her, while subsisting in a 'sea of desperation'. The support we receive, both on a personal and community level can aid us in re-framing our problems, and lead us to seek an alternative solution.

"Where in the bible has this happened? Does God really hear our cry for help?" she asked inquiringly.

"I know you really need answers. Let's go for the prayer and fasting," I pleaded sensitively.

This was a treasured opportunity to resume my research. Sandra sincerely needed answers. But more urgently, she needed relief. In my searching of the Holy Scriptures, I unearthed First Kings 13, which records an episode demonstrating the sympathetic and compassionate character of the God of Heaven: "At the LORD's command, a man of God from Judah went to Bethel, arriving there just as Jeroboam was approaching the altar to burn incense. Then at the LORD's command, he shouted, 'O altar, altar! This is what the LORD says: A child named Josiah will be born into the dynasty of David. On you he will sacrifice the priests from the pagan shrines who come here to burn incense, and human bones will be burned on you.' When King Jeroboam heard the man of God speaking against the altar at Bethel, he pointed at him and shouted, 'Seize that man!' But instantly the king's hand became paralyzed in that position, and he couldn't pull it back. The king cried out to the man of God, 'Please ask the LORD **your** God to restore my hand again!' So the man of God prayed to the LORD, and the king's hand was restored and he could move it again" (I Kings 13:1-2, 4,6, NLT).

The King was so hungry to intercept the divine message that he "was filled with a spirit of defiance against God and attempted to restrain the one who had delivered the message."[63] Notice that although the King disrespected God's prophet and ignored the divine message, at the King's request, God displayed a heart of grace and healed his paralysed hand. The New Living Translation captures the spirited plea of the Israelite King with the Hebrew word for 'cry' *qara*. On realising his plight, the King screamed in desperation begging with tears for healing. It is in our moments of deepest tears that the heart of God is touched with our burdens. In fact, a repentant heart instigates the God of Heaven to respond to our desires.

Furthermore, Scripture affirms that God is a healer, which assures us that He is still omnipotent. "The king of Aram had great admiration for Naaman, the commander of his army, because through him the LORD had given Aram great victories. But though Naaman was a mighty warrior, he suffered from leprosy. One day the girl said to her mistress, 'I wish my master would go to see the prophet in Samaria. He would heal him of his leprosy.' But Elisha sent a messenger out to him with this message: 'Go and wash yourself seven times in the Jordan River. Then your skin will be restored, and you will be healed of your leprosy.' So Naaman went down to the Jordan River and dipped himself seven times, as the man of God had instructed him. And his skin became as healthy as the skin of a young child's, and he was healed!" (2 Kings 5:1,3,10, 14, NLT). Such dramatic stories illustrate how people, within one's community, advocate on other people's behalf, in seeking for divine intervention. The display of community responsibility sparks a sense of hope in our hearts as we focus on the Heavenly One who cares about His created beings. These biblical illustrations demonstrate God's willingness to heal individuals in a public context at their request. Here we notice in each case, the ailing individuals extending the invitation to God's leaders and prophets to invoke the healing power of God.

As I resumed the sensitive topic with the easily-swayed mother-of-three, I noticed her hands outstretched, as if willing to grasp whatever appeared before her.

"How soon are you thinking of starting?" she probed deeply.

"I can start next Monday. I will be at home for that week. I can devote some time praying with you."

"How much time can we spend in this prayer session?'"

"I can set aside the time. Think about it and by the weekend we can decide whether or not we are going for it," I assured her.

"Okay, I will let you know. I need to do something," she replied resolutely.

So often we anticipate a time when we can revert to those special moments we had long ago. It helps us to realise that our present life does not always have to consist of difficulties. But by reflecting on those occasions, we are provided with a sense of hope and comfort. And no matter how deep and wide our wounds are, based on God's will for our lives, we can experience healing through His divine power.

The conversation was about to come to a close that night. As Sandra was about to depart, she quickly slipped into a mood with an air of resignation. Her hope of finding relief seemed to be fading and fluctuating rapidly.

"I'm really concerned about Patricia and Janice. I don't know if I could continue like this. I don't want to waste your time," this vacillating mother finally blurted out.

"Let's go through the week and see what happens," I responded.

I sensed profound uncertainty in her voice. While she made her way back to her car, I realised that tapping into the 'good old days' can be a resourceful way of soothing our wounds. And certainly, we can find inspiration to move on, in expressing sentiments similar to the Psalmist:

> I lift up my eyes to the hills—
>> where does my help come from?
> My help comes from the LORD,
>> the Maker of heaven and earth.
> He will not let your foot slip—
>> he who watches over you will not slumber;
> indeed, he who watches over Israel
>> will neither slumber nor sleep.
> The LORD watches over you—
>> the LORD is your shade at your right hand;
> the sun will not harm you by day,
>> nor the moon by night.
> The LORD will keep you from all harm—
>> he will watch over your life;
> the LORD will watch over your coming and going
>> both now and forevermore.
>
> _____ Psalm 121

Scripture also portrays Yahweh caring about the welfare of His people in ancient times. When we peruse Genesis 29:31, the biblical author informs us that: "When the LORD saw that Leah was not loved, he opened her womb, but Rachel was barren," (NIV). This was in response to the Divine insight where God observed that Jacob "loved also Rachel more than Leah," (Genesis 29:30). So, even though Leah did not explicitly asked for healing, God graciously healed barrenness in private, whereby she "became pregnant and gave birth to a son. She named him Reuben, for she said, 'It is because the LORD has seen my misery. Surely my husband will love me now'" (Genesis 29:32, NIV). Similarly, "God remembered Rachel; he listened to her and opened her womb. She became pregnant and gave birth to a son and said, 'God has taken away my disgrace,'" (Genesis 30:22-23, NIV). No doubt Rachel had been yearning to have children, and even though her healing was done in private, God responded to the invitation and blessed her so that she bore two sons for Jacob. While the public-private debate may exist, we recognise that God is not bound by context. His power transcends invitations or lack thereof, in order to bring wholeness and peace to humanity.

**Thoughts for Action** *[Jot down your responses]*

- What is that past experience or activity that you greatly desire to go back to now ?

- How would this past experience or activity help you in your present situation?

- Share/Write down the level of community responsibility you have benefited from recently?

## Moments of Surrender

- Is there a past experience with which you are in need of help? If writing it out would help, feel free to take you time and do just that here.



- Take some time to reach out to the God of Heaven by openly sharing the details with Him at this moment.

# 6

# Fading Hope

Have you ever attempted to avoid having an encounter with an individual who you have not been getting along with for a while? Perhaps you were sitting in a public place, passing through the church lobby after a worship service, leaving a lecture room at the university or approaching the choir-room door. You unavoidably encounter this person who has neglected you terribly, deceived you or who has offended you at some time. This is an individual you prefer not to face or to interact with in anyway, at least not now. Perhaps it's a workers' meeting, church service or a luncheon when, unexpectedly your eyes make four with this person. Instinctively, you slip through an open door, slide back into your seat, hold the newspaper high to conceal your identity or turn your back to glance at a picture. Or the person may have been relaxing in the living room, but you dash off to the dining room. Or you allow the door of your bedroom to conceal you from making contact with this individual. This is the moment, if no other time, that you are incapable emotionally of addressing the issue. For now, you want to be left alone, rather than fighting a battle for which you are unprepared.

You and I have been there.

It was there that the emotionally tired females of this five-member family found themselves. It was during a school week when two of the girls' own ordeals barred them from attending school. Sandra had worked the night shift. Nevertheless, after rising from her bed late into the day,

Janice spent the part of what was left of her day reading a gripping book. Meanwhile Patricia, who had risen earlier, had taken Judith to school and returned. It was one of those few occasions when Judith went to school. By the time she returned, Janice was engaged in a few television shows and reading her book. Sometime before the children's demanding dad left for work, Janice made a request.

"Can we have some money," she boldly asked.

"Aren't you supposed to be at school? It's time you make the effort and make something of your life. You all have life too easy," dad insisted.

"We may not be at home. We may be going out to the shopping centre with the other young people," she replied.

"If you are not well, you shouldn't be going anywhere. So stay home. And Patricia, don't you forget to collect your sister from school," dad ordered authoritatively

"What do you know? You don't even care about us. So you can't tell me what to do with my life. I wish we didn't have to be here with you. You can't disappear though?" Janice quickly added as she walked out of the room.

"Don't leave this house today," dad shouted out while he left for work.

Janice just shrugged her shoulders. How will Janice respond to her dad's demands, knowing that he hardly supports them during their difficult moments? It was an overcast day with the clouds scattered across the atmosphere. Patches of light could be seen, as the sun tried to shine painstakingly. A chilly breeze blew calmly over the house. The top of the trees struggled to sway. It appeared as if life on the outside of the house was a premium. The vibrant neighbours did not trouble the streets, much less their door locks.

Meanwhile, Sandra, on her way home, had stopped to visit Topane, one of her friends, who was due to travel overseas

"Hi, you're out very early," Topane queried.

"I am now coming off from my night shift. I just stop by to see you before you leave."

"You can have some toast and herbal tea," the caring friend offered.

"O.k."

"Where are the girls?"

"They are at home. Two of them are not able to go to school this week," Sandra shared bravely.

"Have you been checking out anything?"

"I am still looking, but things don't look good," the exhausted support worker added.

"How are things going between yourself and Samuel?"

"I am really struggling with him. He does not support us. I have had enough and the girls are not getting any better," Sandra responded harshly.

"So what are you thinking?" Topane probed further.

"Girl, I need to get some sleep and also check on the girls. We will talk later," Sandra remarked as she made a bee-line for the door.

The Road Safety Campaign promoters in Britain have adopted the slogan "Tiredness Kills". It is in response to many exhausted drivers inevitably sleeping at the wheel while on the motorway. Police and road safety experts firmly contend that sleepiness accounts for at least ten percent of all road accidents and twenty percent of accidents on the motorway. Undeniably, it is considered to claim more lives on public roads than alcohol consumption. In fact, at least 40,000 serious injuries and nearly 3,500 deaths occurred on British roads in 2009, with drowsiness considered to be a major cause. Furthermore, it is very probable that road accidents relating to sleep result in death and serious injury. Experts argue that each death on the road costs over £1 million. Interestingly, most accidents happen in the early hours of the morning and mid-afternoon. It is believed that these time periods are when the body's natural clock is at its low points. A close examination of the data indicates that many of these accidents are work related. Individuals such as trucks and company car drivers become sleepy but often ignore it. Besides, young men, aged 18-30, are mostly at risk.

Having arrived home, Sandra sauntered into the house. She was burdened down with fatigue. She checked on the girls. But being exhausted from the night shift, she crawled into her bed. Fortunately for her, this was her off day. The gold-rim oblong clock on the piano struck one. Physical exhaustion was gnawing on Patricia's body. It overpowered her, thus pushing her to her room. Having barely reached there, she collapsed into her bed and was soon snoring. By now Janice was tired and her eyelids craved for sleep because of the persistent reading and television watching. Instinctively, Janice headed for her bed.

I stop here to ponder for a while. *Didn't Jesus heal many people in his day? What's wrong with us today?* I needed to check this out to have a grasp of Jesus' ministry during his time on earth. From my research of the Scripture, Jesus, in carrying out His mission, "went about all Galilee, teaching in their synagogues, preaching the gospel of the kingdom and healing all kinds of sickness and all kinds of disease among the people" (St. Matthew 4:23, NKJV). Here, Jesus was engaged in a three-fold ministry, that of preaching, teaching and healing as he traversed around His community and among his fellowmen.[64] St. Matthew, the First Evangelist, in describing Jesus' ministry, reported that it was healing, through which individuals with diverse types of diseases and illnesses were made well. Interestingly, the emergence of these various ministries highlight that people had great needs to which Jesus attended.

Anthony Saldarini, in examining Matthew's writing, refers to the biblical narrative in St. Matthew 4:23-25 as a summary [65] of Jesus' extensive ministry in which He engaged after being baptised with water by John the Baptist (St. Matthew 3:14-15) and with the Holy Spirit by God, the Father (St. Matthew. 3:16-17). Moreover, Matthew, the First Gospel writer, in remarking that people brought the sick to Jesus for healing, implies that many were healed publicly. Notably, Matthew recorded a list of sicknesses which emphasise "the necessity and centrality of healing to the work of ancient popular teachers and holy men in the Near East.".[66] With Jesus being involved in various aspects of ministry, we recognise a Christ-centred perspective on these ministries, in that, He initiated these people-centred spiritual activities so that people's anguish can be alleviated.[67]

That afternoon, Patricia had overslept. While everyone was asleep, it drizzled persistently with sleet for about three hours. A few puddles of icy water could be seen in the back yard. A loud clap of thunder stirred Patricia from her slumber. She awoke, stretched and sauntered to the kitchen to have a snack.

"Oops," Patricia thought.

She had forgotten to pick up her sister, Judith, from school. She was left there for over an hour. During that time the school had called Judith's dad. Having remembered, Patricia rushed over to the school to collect her little sister. In about two hour's time, the icy drizzles were the only thing that greeted Samuel as he rushed in out of the persistent sleet.

On seeing Patricia in the kitchen, he inquired sternly,

"Why did you leave your sister at school so late?"

"Oops! I forgot. I overslept," she replied calmly.

"What you mean you overslept. So you mean to say you so lazy you couldn't collect your own sister?" dad retaliated, shouting to the top of his voice.

"I was tired and I dropped off to sleep. What wrong with having a sleep?" Patricia retorted angrily.

"So where is she now?" dad insisted, throwing his attaché case into the long cosy settee.

"She's upstairs in Janice's room watching television."

"Have you checked on her homework?"

"I am hungry and am getting a snack first. I will do it later," Patricia snapped.

By this time the noise, ascending the stairs in the house, had stirred Janice, who rushed down the stairs. The sleet continued to wash the exterior walls of the house. But it brought a cold air into to the living room.

Meanwhile Judith came out of the room and looking over the balcony, overheard the heated conversation. Simultaneously, dad barged angrily into the kitchen and slapped Patricia, as he shouted viciously at her.

"Don't you disobey me, ever."

Janice shouted at her dad. With fiery rage in her bright eyes and bitterness in her heart towards her unsupportive dad, she rushed for a nearby knife and pushed it towards his face.

In a large country in the sub-Asian continent, soldiers have been attempting to eradicate militia and anti-government war fighters since 2001. In the meantime, the population feels threatened by the prevailing gunfire and bomb blasts, events that put them 'on edge'. Even a traffic jam can provoke a comment on this Islamic nation's dismal state, which most people here believe is at its bleakest since international troops assisted the government in toppling the inhumane and power-hungry militia. It's a striking sentiment when you consider it comes after eight years of international intervention, about $60 billion spent in foreign aid and the lives of thousands of foreign troops and civilians lost in such a war.

Hope for a normal country and normal life returning to this Asian state is fading away slowly in spite of the increase in international forces of over 100 000. Ironically, the anti-government soldiers have also swelled in numbers. The battles which were limited to the borders, have invaded nearly every corner of the country, including the frontier-like capital. Situations like these drain the people's hope and quest for a change. In fact, a ray of light shone throughout the country where a vast sea of blown-out buildings in the city has been completely rebuilt. Added to this are multi-storey shopping malls encased in glass symbolising a newfound prosperity, revived travel agencies, internet cafes, and even local fast-food chain outlets. But then, the on-going war continues to ravage lives: local and foreign, pollute the atmosphere and rob residents of a long-sought-after livelihood. Everyone's hope has been fading- and fading rapidly.

Hope is a combination of expectation and desire. Moreover, it is a feeling of trust. And although we cannot touch or hold it, others can see a display of hope on our faces, hear the expectancy in our voice and watch the confidence in our body language. The sanguine individual is buoyant about something happening positively or receiving good news. Living with anticipation leads us to see, taste and smell hope which creates the acronym:

**H**arnessing
**O**pportunities
**P**ractical to our
**E**xistence

Even when the odds appear stacked against us, what we foresee through God's grace and in faith, our conviction and divine inspiration assure us that we can move ahead, knowing that the God of Heaven will accomplish His will in our lives and bring glory to His Majestic Name. When we bring up the subject of hope, we cannot skip the opportunity to ask burning questions: Is your hope alive? Or Fading? What is keeping your hope alive? Or Has your hope dies? For what or whom are you hoping? Is the hope which you have focused on events and achievements at present? Is your hope centred only on the afterlife? Or is your hope caught between achieving success in this present life and experiencing bliss and peace in the new earth and new heaven?

Going back to my research, I found some intriguing details about Jesus' ministry among the people. When we pay closer attention to Jesus' ministry, we may wish to understand it in light of the "Kingdom of God since He focused extensively on this theme on numerous occasions." [68] In St. Mark 1:40-45, Jesus heals a leper at his request and in St Mark 2:1-12 a paralytic, on asking to be healed, is made whole, both of which were done publicly. On the other hand, even though Jesus publicly healed the demon-possessed man in St. Mark 1:21-28 and publicly raised the widow's son at Nain in St Luke 7:11-17, both were done without an invitation. Nevertheless, in reading of Jesus' extensive ministry to the demon possessed, we must understand that this type of ministry demonstrated a struggle between God and an 'enemy', which begun with the temptations in the wilderness and ended triumphantly at the cross.[69]

Apart from the public domain, Jesus also privately raised a ruler's daughter in St Mark 5:21-24. The humanity of Jesus was demonstrated often, as at times when He displayed compassion for individuals. [70] Indeed, we should see His ministry of healing in the context of compassion. It is interesting to note that while the Jewish leaders in Jesus' time were "disputing about the origins and meanings of disease, Jesus takes a pragmatic approach, seeking to cure rather than explain it."[71] Could this not be an indication that Jesus was far less concerned about whether or not he healed people's wounds in private or public? Even though we are aware of the public-private debate, it did not prevent Christ from extending His touch to individuals who were desperate for relief. Indeed, Jesus' willingness to heal individuals whose ray of hope continued to slip from them was not hinged on being invited.

The noise had also stirred Sandra from her coveted sleep. By the time she rushed down the stairs and barged into the kitchen, she encountered Patricia, her raging husband and an anger-infested Janice wielding the knife. Immediately she snatched the knife from Janice's hand and led them out of the kitchen.

"It's time we get out of here," Sandra snarled sharply.

"Who do you think you are? Can't you see that the only thing shining on you is your hair? You don't even deserve to live." the angry dad replied.

"Mummy, he slapped Patricia."

By this time Samuel was trembling and foaming at the mouth. Would this situation trigger an emotional breakdown?

Leading Janice by the hand, mum climbed the stairs in a flash and demanded that everyone got dress and packed a bag.

Meanwhile, Samuel had dialled the police and reported Janice's attack on him.

"We can't stay here tonight," she alerted them.

Having finished packing, they headed for the door and left without a farewell. On opening the door, they were greeted by two male police officers and another lady.

Sandra and Janice's eyes popped open. They seemed to have recognised the lady.

"Are you Sandra?" the lady asked.

"Yes I am."

"And who is Janice?" the lady asked, while the senior police officers looked on sternly.

"Can we go in out of this bad weather?" the leading police officer insisted.

The sleet was still pouring down persistently.

"Good evening, you must be Samuel," the other officer greeted.

"I am afraid we received a report that one of the children pulled a knife on her dad," the leading police officer shared.

"I am a social worker from social services. From our reports at the office, we will have to take her away. Actually she is on the list of children to be placed in a foster home." Janice dropped to the ground in tears. She howled and screamed.

"No mummy, don't let them do it."

Immediately she was led to the police car. It quickly sped away. Sandra, trembling, held onto her other two children. They blocked the icy liquid with their coats and escaped into her car. As they sat there, they pondered for a while. Then Patricia uncontrollably broke down in tears.

"I should have had that knife because I...," Patricia burst out, as she wept.

"Don't you think like that child. He is still your father," mum reminded the eldest daughter in the family.

"Don't wa-annnt to see him. He'ssss a bad m-aan," Judith stammered, while a few tears trickled down her cheeks.

Patricia patted her on the back. Sandra's hope of finding help was fading faster than she had anticipated. Worst yet, her marriage seemed to be developing into a stalemate. How do we regain courage and inner strength when our glimmer of hope escapes our outstretched grasp? It is in these unexpected times that we need to draw on the resources in our community, be they ethnic or spiritual so that we may find comfort for our crushed spirits.

**Thoughts for Action** *[Jot down your responses]*

- Did you ever feel that you were progressing with your situation and then it turned upside down ?

- How did you handle it?

- Share/Write down how you felt when your situation took a different turn?

- What resources do you have that can aid you in regaining hope?

**Moments of Surrender**

- When your ray of hope becomes dark, this can lead to loneliness. Take some time to ask a trusted friend to pray with you.

# 7

# Comforting the Wounded

Sometime in 1993, the members of the Adventurers and Pathfinders Clubs at my local congregation met, as they often did, for teaching sessions and practice in marching and drilling. Every fortnight, the children would meet with their leaders and club teachers to be taught various biblical subjects such as the creation story, aspects of nature and the history of their denominational church among other topics. One quiet afternoon, on completing the sessions, everyone trickled out of the church as they chatted. Out in the street, one of the girls became breathless. The screams from the terrified children attracted the Pathfinders Club Director. She rushed over. It was then that someone alerted her that the girl was having an asthma attack. It was growing worst and she did not have her inhaler.

"Can anyone perform First Aid?" the Club Director inquired.

None of us had First Aid training, not even the director. Immediately she announced,

"We have to take her to the hospital now."

Looking around, she discovered that there were no other cars but mine. She immediately alerted me that I would need to take both she and the girl to hospital. A few strong and able-bodied individuals assisted the ailing girl into the back seat of my red Mitsubishi car. Then the club director jumped in, closed the door and placed the girl on her lap. Immediately, I switched on my hazard lights and rushed to the local hospital which was

30 minutes away from where the incident occurred. It felt weird. My heart was racing faster than the cars in Formula One competitions. We ensured that the little girl was as comfortable as she could and that there was ample ventilation in the car. Every few moments I would glance through my rear-view mirror and ask how she was doing.

In order to arrive as quickly as possible, I had to beep the car horn to overtake slow- and fast-moving vehicles. My hand-foot co-ordination was tested fully. Accelerating. Changing into high and low gears. Manoeuvring parked cars and on-coming traffic. Even approaching traffic lights which showed red, I had no choice. Instinctively, I sounded the horn while looking left and right and then rushed through the danger zone. A little girl lay in the backseat. Her life was on the line. It was a frightening experience, but we managed to reach the hospital safely. As soon as we arrived, she was given immediate priority. We breathed a sigh of relief.

Comforting an individual during a traumatic situation can be overwhelming and apprehensive. Where can these hurting human beings find comfort? There in mum's car, Patricia wiped a tear from her own eyes. She wanted to be there for her trembling little sister. The more she wiped them away, the more the tears brewed in her eyes. Next to her, Judith sobbed continuously.

Each of them was riveted to her seat in the car. Mum stared through the sleet-infested translucent windshield. The icy sleet was steadily pouring down on them. The two sisters huddled together to maintain the warmth that was ebbing. Sandra was contemplating deeply. She was so engrossed with her own thoughts that she forgot to warm up the car. A number of questions rushed through her emotionally-saturated mind. *Where will we sleep tonight? Should I go back into the house? Can Patricia handle this stress any further? Should I go to my mum or my sister?*

"Mum!" Patricia shouted, bringing her bewildered mum back to the situation at hand.

"Wh-wh-errrre are we go-iing?" Little Judith managed to ask.

By now Sandra was lost for ideas. She turned the ignition. There was no response. After a few tries, the 1995 'antique' Rover started. The engine kicked in and they were on their way. They cruised along the road with hayfields on both sides and then turned onto a long stretch of road. They drove for about two miles. And as they made their way towards their 'home', they ended up travelling along a dual carriageway near their neighbourhood. They drove and drove. Night had already set in. The sun had set beyond the horizon some time ago. Cars rushed past them as Sandra drove aimlessly along the hectic carriageway. This compliant and good-natured mum and her girls had just become 'homeless'. Was this a fair deal? How would she be able to handle leaving her life's investment behind? This sudden twist in this family's plight certainly leaves you and me pondering: *With Sandra leaving the matrimonial home, will this cause Patricia to suffer further? Will she have more freedom to seek the help that she longingly needs?*

It was at this moment that I wondered how Jesus' disciples cared for the wounded after He went back to Heaven. Well, so far, I have discovered that divine healing in the New Testament is Christ-directed and Christ-initiated. It is hoped that the teachings, practices and ministerial work of the apostles would serve as a model for the contemporary community of Christian believers. Paul Avis concludes that "In the persons of the Apostles the whole Church is commissioned to exercise a ministry. Its mission takes the form of a ministry involving preaching, baptizing and discipling."[72] However, the importance of the Early Church extends to its teachings regarding the practice of divine healing. The apostles' way of teaching, preaching and practising Jesus' instructions on and the Old Testament perspective on divine healing assist us in gaining interesting insights on raising the wounded.

Prior to analysing the apostles' practices in relation to healing, it would be useful to examine James 5:13-16 to which many Protestant congregations turn for biblical guidance on divine healing. The writer of James, in posing questions about believers' spiritual and physical well-being, advised and commanded believers to initiate the call to the church leaders for receiving divine healing (James 5:14). Moreover, the ministry described in this text is to be "exercised by the recognised elders in the local church, in the context of pastoral care and oversight."[73] The verb *proskaleomai* in the middle voice indicates that the sick individual should summon or invite the church leaders to him/herself, suggesting that the healing service be conducted privately.

In bringing a balanced understanding to the above-mentioned text in the biblical book of James, we should recognize that it refers to "when a person is sick upon his [her] bed, if he [she] calls for the elders of the church, and they carry out the directions in James, anointing the sick with oil in the name of the Lord, praying over him the prayer of faith. … It cannot be our duty to call on the elders of the church for every little ailment we have, for this would be putting a task upon the elders."[74] Such an implication brings about tension between private and public divine healing, seeing that based on the Four Gospels, Jesus conducted divine healing both privately and publicly. Interestingly, for Christ, the public display undoubtedly created a spectacle, thus causing Him to become famous in the neighbouring cities. Apart from this, the invitation/non-invitation tension relating to divine healing also arises. Thus, we are aware that Jesus healed people who specifically asked for it and those who did not call Him, highlighting the fact that Jesus' response to our pain transcends an invitation for healing.

Turning back to the seemingly 'homeless' females of this family, with that trademark tight grin on Sandra's face, she blurted out to the girls,

"Let's go back home."

"No mummy. I don't want to go back there," Patricia insisted.

"We have no choice," mum reminded Patricia.

"You don't care about us. You just like him," Patricia shouted.

With that, they headed back home. Having reached back, the house was pitched black. On entering, Samuel was nowhere to be seen. By now it was time for bed. Mum put Judith to bed and Patricia went off to her room. At approximately 10 O'clock, Samuel arrived. Patricia was still up. She hadn't change. During this time she was scribbling a note to leave on her bed. In fact she was still wearing her overcoat and her handbag lay on her bed. Within an hour Patricia, leaving the note behind, sneaked out and ran off in the dead of the night. She took a bus to Bridgette, her friend and stayed there for the night.

By 7 a.m, Sandra had risen and was making breakfast for Judith. Meanwhile, she shouted for Patricia to wake up Judith. There was no response. Mum ascended the stairs, pushed open the door and saw the note on the bed.

'Dad should not have slapped me. Don' t look for me! I am O.K. Goodbye.'

Having read the note, she confronted Samuel.

"You see how destructive you can be. You don't care about us. Here, read it."

Fortunately, Sandra had another off day from university. She immediately called Patricia's mobile phone. It was as dead as a doorpost. Then she began calling various friends about Patricia's whereabouts. She came up empty-handed because she did not know about Bridgette, a new friend who Patricia had meet some time ago from a different school. Seeing it was time for Judith to go to school, Sandra got dressed, finished prepared her youngest daughter and dropped her off. Instead of returning home, she drove everywhere-back streets, near the church and even through the city centre. There was no sign of Patricia.

By the time she had returned home, Samuel had left for work. Soon after, the telephone rang.

"Hi Sandra, this is Paulette. I just heard that Patricia was at a girl by the name of Bridgette."

"Do you have her number?"

"It is..." she replied.

Being desperate to find her hurting daughter, she dialled the number.

"Hello, is this Bridgette?"

"Yes."

"I am Patricia's mother. Have you seen her?"

"She came here last night and said that she needed somewhere to stay for the night so I allowed her to stay."

"Is she still there?"

"No. She told me that she was going by a guy in Lin n n …."

Mum was furious.

"Lin n n n n …? What for? Do you have a number for him?"

Having written down the number, she dialled it. It was silent. Not even the answering machine cut in to take messages. And there was no more news for the remainder of the day. Sandra's mind was racing at top speed. To keep focused, he tidied the house and performed other house chores. By the time she had completed the house work, it was just after half past three. She rushed off to school, collected Judith and on her way back home, her mobile phone rang. Sandra braked immediately and answered the mobile, thinking that it was Patricia.

"Hi! Is this Sandra? It is Paul from Li n n n... I just want to let you know..."

"Where is my daughter? Send her back now," Sandra screamed.

"Hey, Hey! Don't blame me. I didn't know she had run away. She asked me to let you know she is coming back down, but she's afraid to come home," Paul shared.

Mum ended the call and then put her head on the steering wheel. She then recomposed herself and returned home. That was the last time she heard anything about her eldest daughter for the rest of the day. After giving Judith her evening meal, Sandra packed a bag and jumped into her car with Judith.

"Wh-wh-errrre are we goin' ?" Judith asked with a stammer.

"To Mrs. Bruce's. I can't take any more of this."

The Bruce's home was about half a mile from her street. Mum, on starting the 'ancient' Rover, took off and in a short time, she was pushing the 1995 model with the accelerator. The car pulled up safely outside the Bruce's. As the two occupants disembarked, they stepped into some thick black slush. It almost drew them below its surface like quicksand. They gingerly approached the wooden door. After pressing the doorbell a few times, Mr. Gray appeared at the door, opened it and greeted the guests.

"Sandra and Judith are at the door," Jane, the oldest of Mrs. Bruce's daughter, shouted back to her mother as she beckoned them to enter.

"Who?" Mrs. Bruce queried, as she rushed through the hall way.

"Hi Sis," Sandra greeted Mrs. Bruce with a prolonged tight hug, not wanting to release her motherly friend.

Judith followed Jane and soon took up residence in the living room.

"You didn't tell me you were coming over," Mrs Bruce replied.

They quickly moved into the dining room where Mrs. Bruce was about to prepare for supper. Her husband had already left for work because he was on nights.

"No. I didn't have the time. Everything happened too quickly. Social Services came and took Janice away. And this morning Patricia ran away. She won't call. Somebody called early saying that she said that she was O.K. But I am worried.

"How comes? Why did they take Janice away?"

"The children said that he slapped Patricia and Janice rushed for whatever came to her hand to defend her sister. The noise woke me up from sleeping."

Mrs. Bruce was moved to tears. She shook her head unbelievably.

"Is this justice? What are you supposed to do now?" Mrs. Bruce remarked between her tears.

"I have made up my mind. It's over."

"What could have happened to cause...?" Mrs Bruce inquired, as she sobbed.

"I am up to my neck. Bills. Problems with Janice and now Patricia," Sandra admitted.

"... her to turn on him?" She probed in a pondering mood.

"We can't go back to that house. I need a new environment. We are not getting the help that we really need. It looks as though nobody can help, or want to help," Sandra shared frustratingly.

"When last did you speak with your friend? I'm sure he would be willing to pray with you and help you through this situation," the insightful, caring mother-of-four suggested, as she wiped her tearful eyes.

We too learn from such debilitating incidents how members of our own community can let us down and even disappoint us. We expect a better response from those of our own household, ethnic groups or profession. Yet so often we feel cheated. In the end, we can become disheartened and disillusioned. A spirit of inferiority overshadows us. And especially when we are wounded, we feel as though he wounds have been widened. Such is the time we need to be comforted. We have an inner need to be loved and to have a sense of belonging. But it's our divinely-activated faith, inner boldness and determination that drive us to overcome our circumstances.

The caring attitude of this mother-of-four, who has been mourning the death of her three children, reminds me of a familiar story. A matured Jewish man was on his way from Jerusalem, Israel's Capital city, to Jericho, a Palestinian city near the River Jordan. As he travelled purposefully and briskly along the Palestinian West Bank, a gang of angry-looking armed robbers attacked him mercilessly. It was a calm day. The wind blew across the Jordan Valley intermittently. Hardly anyone took this route to traverse between Israel and Palestine. As the Israeli hurriedly moved ahead, the defiant and deviant men who were wearing hoodies, baggy pants and carrying knives, pounced on him. They pitilessly threw him to the ground, slapped him, kicked him, ripped his clothes off him and beat him until he bled. There was blood everywhere. It oozed from his head, nose, ears and mouth.

The desire to complete his trip had now faded into oblivion. He groaned. Cried. Wailed. But in such a lonely and deserted place, it was certain that no one would hear him. So they left him there to perish. 'Out of the blue' a parish priest took the same route, perhaps to deliver the weekly

Sacrament to his parishioners. He was neatly dressed and well-groomed. And although the long brightly-decorated robe he wore weekly would cover any dirt on his suit, he was very careful about getting his clothes soiled with dirt or even the wounded man's blood. The wounded man, full of bruises, cuts and lacerations, was losing blood by the hour. He could hardly groan much less beckon for assistance.

Being fully occupied with reaching the Cathedral early, the self-conceited priest scornfully glanced at the dying man and rushed over, at a 45-degree angle, on the other side of the road to avoid getting involved. Fear must have riveted his mind at that instance. Fear of suffering a similar fate. Fear of giving of his own resources to help the dying man. He was in no mood to show compassion nor to bring comfort to the weak, marginalised, afflicted or the vulnerable. In fact, even though his role required him to perform such pastoral duties, he was captivated by other interests. Time was ticking away. He didn't even stop to consider that this dying man could be one of his parishioners. In fact most dying individuals often call for their priest. Could this man have been calling out lamentably for his parish priest?

Soon after, a Curate, the parish priest's assistant, rushed by. He was pre-occupied with trying to live up to his reputation of arriving at the Cathedral punctual to assist with the preparations for the church service. By now the blood had trickled down the pathway. The curious curate spotted the red liquid. He came near, had a look at his gaping wounds and shook his head in pity. He wished in his heart that he could stay with him. But his head was in control-he needed to be early for the special church service. So, with his compassionate heart pounding with profound conviction, he stepped over the bleeding victim and rushed on to his destination.

After some time, the dying man's groans faded into partially audible and fainting whispers. By now the blood had thickened. Soon after, a hated and despised individual from a minority ethnic group was riding his donkey along this solitary and secluded route. On spotting the thick dark liquid in his path, he halted the faithful animal and immediately jumped off. He fell to the ground beside the wounded man. And when he saw the extent of his wounds, he sighed deeply. He looked to the heavens, as if to ask: why did the God of Heaven allow this to happen? Life is not fair. Often times, we are dealt a harsh 'hand' in the arena we play out this life. It's the vulnerable, marginalised, outcast and the weak that often suffer. Justice seems to pass them by, especially when they lack the financial resources. Injustice makes us become distrustful in the social, political and judicial systems of society. At times anger sets in and we want to take out our frustrations on others or on the superstructures in society. Sometimes we damage government property, litter the streets or even refuse to abide by some of the laws. At other times, we feel as though the system is crushing us and there is no help.

The old adage, 'every dog has its day' was fitting for this occasion. In fact, the dying man's moment had finally appeared. The stranger engaged in wound therapy by removing the clots of blood, bandaging the wounds and giving the victim some refreshing liquid. Then he carefully lifted him on to his donkey, while he was still wearing his blood-stained trousers. As the stranger walked alongside his donkey, he chatted with his 'patient' to lift his spirit and take his mind off his plight. Since he did not have the appropriate medicine and equipment to take care of this weak traveller fully, he stopped at the first inn and paid for his stay and medical care. Do we determine who should benefit from our resources based on their ethnicity, social class or the ability to pay back? How should we treat the wounded, be they from our community or not? How should we respond when we hear the desperate plea of a friend, church member, or colleague? Where do we turn when those who have been entrusted with the role of comforting us, turn away from us instead?

I now turn back to the conversation between Sandra and her friend. Having accepted the advice of her trusted friend, the 'homeless' mother-of-three surrendered:

"Let me call later."

It was around 9 p.m when Sandra's mobile phone rang. She scrambled to unzip her handbag. And then she rumbled through the contents to find the phone.

"Hello!"

"Where are you, now?" Samuel demanded.

"Why do you want to know? This is the first time you called me in weeks. I am not coming back there."

"Have you heard anything about my daughter?"

"She hasn't called."

"Mum-mmm-y, is th-aaat Pat?" Judith asked, interrupting.

"No dear. Your father!"

"It's almost a day that she has been missing. Have you called the police?" dad inquired.

"You forget that you have to wait until 24 hours."

"Well, it's almost that now. You should call. And get home before it gets later."

Sandra felt the need to call. About twenty minutes later she called my mobile phone.

"Hello!" I answered.

"Hi, good evening."

"Hi Sandra! Good to hear you?"

"I need to see you urgently. Can I come over and see you either Wednesday or Thursday?"

"What time are you thinking? I am working tomorrow."

"What time would you be back?" she queried.

"I should be back by 4:30 p.m."

"I could come about 6:00 p.m."

"That should be fine. We can meet at my home," I assured her.

It was getting close to bedtime for everyone. The two exhausted mothers were in deep thoughts. Since Mrs. Bruce only had a three-bedroom house, she pondered on how to allocate the beds for the night. Meanwhile,

Sandra's mind flashed on the girls. Suddenly, a high-pitch scream emanated from the living room where the girls had been sleeping soundly.

"A kn-iiii-f-e! A kn-iii-f-e! A kn-i-f-e" little Judith repeatedly shouted.

Jane, who was half asleep in the settee, woke up startled. The two mothers, weighed down with physical and mental exhaustion, rushed into the girls. Sandra pounced on her baby daughter. It was a nightmare. Everyone congregated around trembling Judith. Her hands were shaking with fright. Her eyes of fire conveyed inner fear. The prolonged turmoil in her parents' home was beginning to affect her. We perceive a community spirit in the response of these individuals. It's a spirit that seeks to support hurting individuals by bringing comfort and showing compassion to them. All too often, it is the unlikely hero, the unexpected individual, who shows up on time. In fact, a close-knitted community will consider its members to be neighbours. And this identity leads us to take on our responsibility without focusing on the boundaries of class, ethnicity or education. Such an attitude contributes to the wounded being encouraged and lifted up as opposed to being broken down.

**Thoughts for Action** *[Jot down your responses]*

- To whom did/could you turn in your weakest moment?

- Was this person an unlikely hero or unexpected individual?

- Were you shocked by the response you receive?

• How have your wounds been helped by this response?

**Moments of Surrender**

• Take some time to reflect on the unexpected help you receive/lack of help.

# 8

# Break Down

The Rover 200 model car back in 1995, came with petrol and diesel engines, with 1.4- 1.6- and 2.0-litre capacity. Later the 1.1- and 1.8-litre range of cars was added to the market. The 1995 model's body styles were 3- and 5-door hatchback family car. With a competitive spirit, the manufacturers aimed to cater to the public's needs by rolling off cars with 4-speed automatic and 4-speed manual engines. In order to compete with other car manufacturers during that era, the designers injected 73 horsepower into the 200 model which came with a top speed of 103 miles per hour. To ensure that it was one of the top cars, the makers boosted it with a 41-mile per gallon economy rate and completely re-designed the interior and dashboard to accommodate a passenger airbag in line with new safety standards. Between 1996 and 1998, the third generation 200 was so popular that it became Britain's seventh best selling new car.

Sandra, who was driving for almost three years, had bought a 1995 Rover a year before we had met. But with these powerful car specifications, she would be standing tall and boasting about her 'baby', as she called it. Having owned it for the past fifteen months, she felt safe travelling in her reliable three-door car. Although the car did not give her any cause to be concern, she began worrying about how much longer it could go on. She stared at the keys. Her worries intensified since she was faced with a mountainous life-long mortgage and infrequent medical bills for the girls.

On top of these, there was the house to be maintained. *Could she keep up with all of this? Would she be able to cope? How much longer can she go on like this?*

Judith sprang up out of her nightmare. She looked around at the sea of people who had encircled her.

"Mum-mmm-y, Jan-Jan-ice was bad," she asked.

"You'll be O.K.," mum assured her with a cuddle.

Mrs. Bruce allowed Sandra to occupy the middle-size bedroom for her and Judith. And with the distressed mother-of-three besides her daughter, they spent the night in peace. Everyone slept like a lark. By the time everyone arose from his/her night's slumber the next day, it was almost mid-morning. The girls were already down stairs watching television. By the time Sandra helped the hostess with her chores, it was half eleven.

"I need to report that Patricia is missing."

She took out her mobile phone and made contact with someone on 999.

"Good morning. I am calling to report that my daughter went missing more than a day now," Sandra indicated.

"What is your address? We will send someone over to yours in a few minutes."

"10 Spurs Drive."

Having ended the call, Sandra alerted her friend that she had to go to meet the police at her home. She got Judith ready and both of them headed for the door.

"I'll be back later," Sandra reminded her friend.

In forty minutes, the 'ancient' car had arrived safely. They hadn't put their bags down before a police car pulled up outside. There was a knock on the door.

"Hello!" Sandra said

"Good morning! Are you Sandra?" the senior police officer asked.

"When last did you see your daughter?"

"Tuesday night about 9 p.m"

"What is her name?"

"Patricia."

"What was she wearing when you last saw her?"

Well, it was late into the night and we all had gone off to bed. So I don't know what she was wearing," mum confessed.

"Is there anyone who you think she may have gone by?" the female officer asked.

"I have called all her friends that I know."

"Leave it with us."

By four O'clock, Sandra realised that she wouldn't be able to make the appointment so she called to reschedule. The phone rang.

"Hello!" I said.

"Hi! It's me. Can we put back the appointment until next Monday evening? Something has come up suddenly," Sandra informed me.

"It should be O.K."

Within a second of putting the receiver down, the phone rang again. Looking at the screen, Sandra recognised Patricia's number. Her hands trembled. Her heart was racing. A few thought raced through her mind. *What should I say to her? Will she come back home? Does she hate me?*

"Mum. I don't want you to be mad at me. But I don't want to come back home," Patricia stated.

"Don't say that. You've got to come home. I can't lose Janice and you too. Don't do this to us. Remember you little sister, Judith. She has been asking for you."

"I want my freedom. I am big enough," Patricia demanded.

"Would you please come home? We can sort that out," mum pleaded.

"I can't."

"Where are you now?"

"Near the bus station."

"I will come and get you. Stay there."

Mum alerted Judith to put on her coat and shoes. Then they rushed into the city centre to locate Patricia. In about twenty minutes, Sandra spotted Patricia leaning against a wall near the market. She tooted the horn. Her unkempt daughter scampered over the other side of the road and jumped into the car.

Having arrived back at home, mum hugged her once 'lost' daughter and fed her.

"I hope you know we have to call the police to let them know that we have found you,"

Later in the evening after Sandra had called the police, two police offers responded to the new information. Having arrived, the female officer checked with Patricia to ensure that everything was O.K with her and then they left. Later Patricia went to her room and spent the remainder of the night there. Guilt was eating away at her mind.

"I shouldn't have done that. I was really silly. But he had no right to hit me." Patricia quietly uttered to herself.

As the days passed by, Patricia felt uneasy at home. Her dad continued to 'eye' her, while being silent. The first she had returned to school for a while, Patricia was engaged in a group activity with four other children. They were busy with the task and as they were about to complete it, Patricia collapsed in the on the floor. The more the teacher fanned her, the worst she grew. The teacher sent for the first aider which didn't help. After calling the ambulance, the teachers asked her mother to meet the ambulance at the hospital. After carrying out a number of checks, the female doctor was unable to pinpoint the cause. She prescribed a set of iron tablets for the condition and discharged her.

By the time the next day had arrived, Sandra was unhappy with the latest situation in her home. She needed help with her home situation and the children. Around 5:30 p.m, mum hustled the girls into the car and set off for her destination. On waiting for her to embark on the 12-mile trip, you are probably wondering like me, if the trip will be worthwhile and if the trainee student would encourage this hurting mother to stay in the matrimonial house for the sake of the marriage.

Overnight, the much accumulated sleet slowly condensed, leaving scattered pools of water here and there. With the roads being wet and slippery, drivers were controlling their 'machines' with caution. After travelling some ten minutes, the ageing car gave a sudden jerk. It gave off some thick black smoke that darkened the already dark atmosphere. Sandra became concerned.

"Don't let me down now," she whispered to the Rover, caressing the handle.

A strange noise was emerging from the exhaust pipe while it gave off more of the black stuff. Thinking that the huge puff of black smoke was the car's means of communicating, Sandra pacified the 'antique' vehicle,

"Come on baby. You have never let me down."

Almost a century ago, the word got out that a dependable and trustworthy ship will be setting sail. The *Royal Mail Ship (RMS) Titanic*, which was the largest passenger steamship in the world at that time, set off on her maiden voyage. The 882-foot powerful machine pushed off from Southampton, England on its way to New York City on 10 April 1912. This monstrous vessel, reaching 175 feet towards the sky, was an Olympic-class passenger liner, constructed at the Harland and Wolff shipyard in Belfast, Ireland (now Northern Ireland).

The experienced, qualified and seasoned Lieutenant, Captain Edward J. Smith gave the sailing command and the ship, on spouting out gallons of water from the under-water propellers, set sail with 2,223 people on board. With room for 3 547 holiday-seeking passengers and 860 crew members, she was below her capacity. The 159 coal burning furnaces that fired the 29 boilers made it possible for the ship to travel at a top speed of 23 knots or 26 mph on the seas.

Some of the most experienced engineers designed *Titanic*. And to ensure reliability and safety, the designers some of the most advanced technologies available at the time. Apart from the construction, the special vessel displayed expensive amenities and luxurious features such as sunlit verandas, libraries and barber shops in the first- and second-class areas. Added to these features, the ship carried 20 lifeboats of varying lengths and capacities.

On Saturday night, April 14, 1912, the temperature had dropped to near freezing, inspite of a calm ocean, invisible moon and clear sky. Four days into the crossing, in mid-Spring, the 46 000-ton multi-cylinder-engine vessel struck an iceberg in the middle of the North Atlantic Ocean. About 20 minutes before midnight, the two lookouts ferried danger signals to the bridge. On receiving the life-threatening message 'iceberg right ahead', The First Officer immediately ordered a sudden halt to the massive ship. With an emergency on his hands, his command may have been futile because the dangerous iceberg clipped the right side of *Titanic*.

As the lifeboats were being prepared to be filled with overwhelmed passengers, distress calls and signals pierced the international airwaves. Various ships responded to the emergency. Forty minutes after midnight, 6 lifeboats were lowered from *Titanic*. However, this proved unsatisfactory as the Atlantic waters continued to devour the ships and distressed human beings. At 2:20 the following morning, 1,517 people perished in one of the deadliest peacetime maritime disasters in history. It was around 4:10 a.m, when RMS *Carpathia* arrived in the area, after steaming at 17.5 knots for just under four hours. The herculean trip resulted in many survivors being rescued from the chilly lifeboats.[75]

It's a familiar pattern. The things and people we believe would not let us down, turn out the opposite. We hope that reliability would be a readily available quality possessed by most people, machines and equipment. And we anticipate that the warranty on various products would outlive the commodity. Unfortunately, if they haven't harnessed it, then it wouldn't show up. Whether it is circumstances, the inevitable or a sheer bad attitude towards people, some individuals cannot be counted on in our moment of greatest need. And so do things, be they animals, equipment or vehicles.

How many of us can identify with Sandra at this time? How many of us at some point in our life have been let down by someone or something? We can reminisce on that moment of great, if not greatest, need. Perhaps it was a time when we had to submit the final proof-read thesis. Or, to get on our way for graduation, after working tirelessly for four years. It was that moment when the supposedly reliable turned out to be unreliable and short of integrity. We experience unfaithfulness and that person or thing felt no obligation to us. Such are the episodes that leave us in the 'cold' feeling bewildered, nervous and overwhelmed.

By now Sandra was feeling a sense of betrayal from her car. She urgently needed help for her children. Any kind of help: from God, man or beast. So, on realising that the soft treatment she was dishing out did not encourage her 'baby' to respond favourably to her, she frantically pushed the choking car with the accelerator. It puffed and jerked its way along the isolated dual carriageway. There was no way that she would stop now. It was unthinkable. This carriageway was too dark and lonely. It was cold and there was no guarantee that she would get mechanical assistance from any passer-by.

"It's time to get rid of the old thing," advised Patricia with a giggle in the backseat.

"It's muu-mm's 'ba-ba-by'? Judith added

The determined Sandra glanced through the rear-view mirror with a smile. Then she shook her head. Amidst the jokes and laughter, the Rover rolled onto St. Paul's Road, having travelled the full twelve miles and finally cruised into the driveway.

It was around 6:30 p.m when Sandra and the girls showed up. I waited for them at the entrance, after which I led them to a quiet area. As they sat, mum looked at me as if to say 'I don't know where to start'.

"What was your day like, Patricia?" I inquired.

"Actually, that's why we came to see you. We had a few awful days."

"We?" Patricia asked surprisingly.

"Well, tell him, then," mum suggested.

"What was it like, Patricia?" I probed.

"My dad and I had an argument...," she replied breaking down in tears.

"I came down the stairs and saw Janice with an instrument," mum shared, shaking her head.

"Where is Janice?" I asked.

"Gone to a foster home?" Mum shared

"Why? What happened?

"Because she had a sharp instrument pointing at him, her father called the police. Remember the social worker had been seeing her before. So they took her away. And then this young lady ran away in the middle of the night and only came back yesterday," Mum informed me.

It felt like a dagger. Patricia, being reminded of the incident, broke down in tears. She leaned on her mum's already tired shoulders. That sharp and tense encounter was probably haunting her.

"He doesn't care about us. He is always bossing us around," Patricia pushed, with the tears gushing down her checks.

"What were you thinking when you left home and didn't come back?" I asked.

"I don't think we can go back to that house. Not with him being there," mum added supportively.

I bowed my head in meditation. *Do I have the resources? What can I do to help this family?* I pondered.

"Let me share a text with you. Let's look at St. John 16:33."

Turning to the text, it reads: "I have told you these things, so that in me you may have peace. In this world you will have trouble. But take heart! I have overcome the world" (NIV). I shared the following thoughts with the family. *We live in a world of sin, controlled by the devil and he is the ruler of this world. This is why we struggle so much in this life. I hear your pain and frustration. But I want to encourage you not to lose faith in God. Actually, He says in Him we will have peace. This type of peace will protect our thoughts and guard our minds. That is why God has promised to keep us in prefect peace so that our minds does not become muddled with all sorts of issues. Even though we will have trouble in this world, and be pressured, I want to encourage you be bold because you have victory in God.*

When I reflect on this biblical text, even now, I cannot help by agree with Herman Ridderbos that Christ "confronts them [His disciples] with the reality that is now coming towards them. But he does so not to take from them the confidence of faith that possesses them but to make them understand that their faith will be severely tested." [76] From a Christian worldview, we cannot escape the spiritual attacks hurled at us through human agents. In fact, we are often bombarded with afflictions and distressing circumstances, that we experience "permanent hostility" while we live in this present world.[77] Thus, such ordeals highlight the urgent need for the members of our communities to be faithful to the wounded in their hour of need.

"Thank you," Patricia replied.

"By the way, are we still continuing with the bible studies?" I asked

"Let's put it on hold. Too much is happening," her mother replied.

I earnestly pleaded with God for this family, asking Him to bring peace into their lives and to open a way for them according to His will.

The load which Sandra bore led me to recount my struggle with a yearning desire for my psychiatrically-ill mother to be healed. The first opportunity to take on the role of being responsible for my mother occurred when I was age fourteen. After she was admitted to hospital, I frequently visited her to spend some time with her and to carry clothes for her. During a conversation I had with the nurse-in-charge one afternoon, she remarked,

"For your age, you really have broad shoulders."

The harsh treatment of life, constant hospitalisation, the injections and other types of medication all took a toll on her body and mind. She was not the mother I had known previously. Her hands constantly shook, her lips trembled profusely and her gait had been altered tremendously. As time progressed, she resumed some sense of normality, including returning to her job as a janitorial worker.

On many occasions I wondered how I could find help for this destructive illness that brought instability to her life and certainly to mine. I longed for the time when she would regain her health fully. And throughout the twenty years of her illness, my childhood and young adulthood journeys were riddled with pain, disappointments, family difficulties and unexpected surprises. On becoming aware of my mother's illness, I found myself living in moments of fluctuation. Many days I wondered: *Will she die like this before getting better? Will I ever get back my real mother? Is there no way out of this for her?* I wrestled with a lack of community spirit, an absence of relief and poor familial support. All I wanted was relief for her. And so did Sandra for her daughter.

Tuesday evening arrived. We were still having the youth discussion sessions. It was cold. The wind bit through the pullover and so I had to pull out the warm winter coat. It was about 6:30 p.m that night when I jumped into my 1985 red Golf. It was a reliable machine, at least so far. And although one passenger's door could not open, it allowed me to travel comfortably from point A to B without any alarms. My moment of disappointment however, soon arrived. I was about one mile from the church, where I normally conduct the bible discussion sessions. There at the traffic lights, the small engine cut out. After turning the ignition several times, it kicked in and I was on my way. Five minutes after, it cut out again. Unfortunately, it would not restart. I was too near the church to cancel the studies. The youth were waiting. I could not let them down like my car did to me. I closed up the windows, locked all the doors and walk the remainder of the way. I reached there about ten minutes late, but the youth were happy to see me.

Having finished the studies, I rushed back to the scene of my stalled car. A few of the young people accompanied me on the isolated street. I jumped in and turned the key. There was no 'juice'. After about fifteen minutes, I decided to leave it overnight and call the mechanic. Soon after, Curtis ensured that his passengers arrived home safely and then he ferried me home. The days had rushed by unannounced. The mechanic arrived, checked the ancient car and then pronounced it 'dead'. I became numb with desperation.

"Can't it be revived?" I asked.

"It doesn't worth the money," the mechanic advised.

Looking at my treasured earthly possession, I finally surrendered.

"You need to call a scrap company to take it away for you," the elderly mechanic reminded me.

I accepted that the car had to be scrapped. On locating a scrap metal company, I reservedly handed the car over to him. I felt as though my unborn child had been ripped from me. The sudden and rapid occurrence of events left a vacuum. Life is replete with events that create holes in our family life, finances, hearts and relationships. To close the hole can be painful, but through prayer and a willingness in individuals to be transformed, such holes can be closed.

On the next weekend, I noticed that Sandra and her family were missing from the morning services. However, they managed to make it to the afternoon service. The programme had started with praise and worship session and a prayer session. Soon after, the speaker took to the podium and began to preach. Immediately, there were noises at the back of the church. It was Patricia. She had collapsed again. Luckily, a few of her friends recognised that she was not well and they held her before she could hit the ground. After taking her into the back room of the church, her mother and a few individuals with medical backgrounds were unable to detect the problem. *What could have caused these collapses? Was she sick? Was she hiding something? Taking drugs unknown to her parents? Or was she involved in some other activity?*

Having absorbed the experiences of this family so far, what circumstance has broken you? Are you feeling overwhelmed by the brokenness that may exist in your life? Have you contributed to someone being broken? Are you a reliable member of your community? Taking on appropriate responsibility? Comforting the wounded? Feeling obligated to assist the vulnerable, weak and obscure people in your community? I assure you that in such moments it is possible to echo the sentiments like David, the biblical character:

> Hear my cry, O God,
>     Listen to my prayer.
> From the ends of the earth I call to you,
>     I call as my heart grows faint;
>         Lead me to the rock that is higher than I.
> For you have been my refuge,
>     A strong tower against the foe.
>
> _____ Psalm 61:1-3 (NIV).

When we reflect on our ordeals and those of others, we would agree that some situations cannot be revived. And even if they are revived, they are not the same as at the beginning. Broken hearts, damaged relationships or emotionally-starved people cannot experience healing and reconciliation in a minute, with one counselling session or by a single prayer. Very often, time becomes a healer. We are aware that the journey may be long, but the wait is worth it.

## Thoughts for Action *[Jot down your responses]*

- What situation threatens your pursuit of help for your situation?


- How possible is it/was it to achieve the resources and help that you urgently need?

- How did you cope/ are you coping with or without the resources?

## Moments of Surrender

- As you reflect now, are you aware of any brokenness in your life? Think through it for a moment and look at all your options.

# 9

# The Trip that Turned the Tide

In their height of the 1969 summer, the National Aeronautics and Space Administration (NASA) in America successfully launched a lunar expedition to the Moon from Florida. Since the beginning of the 1960s, the US administration, with President John F. Kennedy at the helm, yearned hungrily to despatch a man successfully to the Moon. The decade had almost ended before this long-sought-after goal could be achieved. But America realised its dream of being a superpower in space exploration. On that historic July 20, Apollo 11 was the first manned mission to land on the Moon with Astronaut Neil Armstrong leading, along with his fellow astronauts: Michael Collins and Edwin 'Buzz' Aldrin. This phenomenal exploration resulted in the first human beings stepping onto the surface of the Moon. An estimated 500 million people worldwide watched this event, the largest television audience for a live broadcast at that time.

The trip became a momentous occasion for inhabitants of the Planet Earth. Ever since then, this memorable trip turned the tide in American space exploration, technological advancement, scientific discoveries, politics and economic policy.

Focusing on Patricia's illness, it felt like ages. She was unable to rejoin the congregation. As I looked outside, I saw the flashing blue lights. Someone had called the ambulance. She spent a lengthy time with the paramedics. However, by the end of the service she was doing well. There was no need to take her to hospital.

One afternoon, I received the application forms and advertising material for an annual prayer and bible conference sponsored by our denominational church. Having experienced powerful and inspiring moments at the previous programmes, I advised the leader to seek for sponsorship for the youth to attend this weekend programme. By the time the weekend had arrived, I had the details to share with them. Sometime after the evening youth service, I summoned all of them together.

"I just received some details about a prayer conference and I would like to invite all of you to it," I shared.

"What is a prayer conference?" Curtis asked inquisitively.

"It's a weekend programme for young people when they spend time studying the bible, worshipping and engaging in different forms of prayer."

"Is that all?" Yolanda demanded.

"On the Saturday night the youth engage in praise and worship, singing choruses until late into the night. Then there is an agape feast the Sunday evening and an anointing service to top it off. It is usually powerful. I don't think any of you should miss this."

"How much does it cost?" Julian asked.

"Twenty pounds per person," I replied.

"That sounds exciting. Let's all go. We would have to hire a coach or bus," Alex suggested with a smile.

"I wonder how helpful it would be for the Patricia?" Sandra queried with a concerned look.

"Which section of the weekend are you talking about?" I inquired.

"Well, I was just thinking how it would benefit Patricia with her issues. Do you think it would help?" Mum pushed.

"If nothing else the anointing service is always a special time. It is usually very powerful," I re-assured her.

"I would really like to experience it," Patricia added.

"Are we all willing to go?" I probed.

"Let's discuss it some more," Sophia suggested.

"And what is the venue?" Patricia asked.

"Grange Castle," I pointed out.

"I know where to find that is. That's a good place to go for trips and sightseeing," Curtis announced.

*Will they really go? Will they find it boring? What if it doesn't turn out the way I described it?* I contemplated. Although these are my thoughts, I am sure you are wondering how this trip will be the answer to this family's health problems. The fact that Sandra had been searching for an appropriate relief for the children's emotional and physical ailments, it was highly probable that she would take this opportunity.

On the next weekend, Curtis took some of most of the young people for a walk to a nearby park after the youth programme had ended at church. The sun was still beaming its rays through the clear crystal azure sky. Flocks of birds gracefully glided overhead in unison. They were neatly aligned in the atmosphere as if held by special glue. The trees and bushes swayed vibrantly in the Northern wind that rippled through the branches powerfully. Mums and dad took strolls with their babies and toddlers. A few people endeavoured to absorb the scarce sunlight by walking around half clad. The youth all gathered around on the scarce vacant benches available.

"Hey, guys. I think we should think seriously about going," instructed Alex

"You know, I wonder if they will perform the anointing session privately like how it is done at people's homes or at church" Julian pondered.

"Do you think that would be a problem?" asked Yolanda.

"Is it biblical?" Julian continued, looking worried.

"Why are you always stirring up trouble? Are you a bible scholar?" Patricia shouted at Julian, while gesticulating with her right hand.

By inspiring and encouraging each other to attend this special prayer conference, these passionate and vivacious young people were displaying a sense of community responsibility. Here we recognise the practical application of Galatians 6:2, which reads: "Carry each other's burdens, and in this way you will fulfil the law of Christ" (NIV). I recognise that the word 'carry' has a far-reaching meaning in that it denotes the idea of supporting and sustaining each other. Of all the variant meanings, this one fits well. We see how critical it is to be there for others. Our mere presence, prayerfully interceding for someone or enquiring about each other's welfare, are all part of us demonstrating our obligation to members of our community. We are there with the individual, silent at times, but also verbally interacting with them. Being present with the hurting, signals ours willingness to 'carry' that individual while they seek for deliverance. By actively engaging with such individuals, we are helping them to find comfort for their pain and burdens. By doing this, through the aid of the Holy Spirit, they can experience comfort and by extension, freedom from the various difficulties we may be facing.

When we reflect on the word 'burden', it denotes a carrying a weight or a heavy load. Let's examine how it fit into the rising passion that the youth had been displaying. Certainly, Sandra and her family were weighed down with emotional, psychological and even physical burdens. The boiling pressure in her home had reached its crescendo. And these thoughtful and considerate young people pensively sensed this family's yearning search for relief from the marital strain and emotional stress.

It's heart-wrenching to be weighed down with burdens, seeing that they impose hardships and a feeling of anxiety on us. In our efforts to get our burdens lifted, at times they feel like an octopus-like albatross tightly secured around our necks. Think for a moment about that burden that you had been weighed down with or that you are oppressed by at present. Was it easy for you? Did you have access to resources? How did you manage during the ordeal? What thoughts swirled around in your head? Divorce? Separation? Suicide? Take an overdose? Murder? Run away from home forever? Or sign yourself into a psychiatric institution? Some burdens can be overwhelming, oppressive, wearisome and exhausting, to the point that they drain us of our inner energies and spiritual faith. Can you see the need for us to demonstrate community and even personal responsibility towards the weak and hurting?

In those moments when we are pressured with burdens, they have the tendency to weaken us. Our emotional resources are weakened, our spiritual faith is weakened and we even feel physical weak. Here is where The Apostle Paul's instructions to the community of Christian believers in Thessalonica become applicable: "Brothers and sisters, we urge you to warn those who are lazy. Encourage those who are timid. Take tender care of those who are weak. Be patient with everyone" (1 Thessalonians 5:14, NLT). On looking at this verse, no doubt like me, you are attracted to the command: 'Take tender care of those who are weak.'

Let's turn our focus for a while on the theological motif of weakness and its derivatives such as 'weak' and 'weaken'. These linguistic terms conjure up imagines of fading, subsiding, being feeble and feeling powerless. You would agree with me that we have at some point in our lives, uttered a similar sentiment like this one: "Have mercy on me and be gracious to me, O Lord, for I am weak (faint and withered away); O Lord, heal me, for my bones are troubled" (Psalm 6:2, AMP). It echoes our cry for release, for deliverance and for a respite from our moments of distress and tribulation. However, Scripture assures us of divine assistance during our spiritual journeys: "Strengthen the weak hands and make firm the feeble and tottering knees" (Isaiah 35:3, AMP). This is an example of God being intentional about lifting us up and empowering us to face life's challenges. Can you not hear him being passionate about giving you deliverance? Can you not hear the urgency in His command? Can you not see His eyes are focused on a particular group of people in this text? Can you hear his heart yearning for the downtrodden, oppressed and those who buckle under the load of emotional, physical and spiritual pressure?

When you survey the Scriptures closely, you will recognise that certainly, God has a vested interest in the life of weak individuals. On reading Isaiah 40:29 in the *Amplified Bible* version that "He gives power to the faint and weary, and to him who has no might He increases strength [causing it to multiply and making it to abound]", you cannot help but sense that tenderness in God's voice.[78] It is in such verses that you can find God. He sees your weakness. He literally gives you power. And He ensures that your endurance does not run out. Actually, one can almost imagine God despatching angels to uphold us when we become debilitated by the pressures in this life. Take courage while travelling on your journey!

Becoming weak is inevitable. It occurs in different spheres of life. We experience powerlessness in our family during a death. Those who are profoundly touched by the death of a loved one tend to grieve longer and more intensely. Others, buckle under the weight of sorrow at the sight of the coffin being lowered into the grave. Traumatic situations such as sexual abuse, fatal car accidents, kidnapping or witnessing violent and brutal killings of human beings render us enfeebled. In relation to the psychological impact of traumatic events on individuals, Babette Rothschild asserts firmly "That traumatic events exact a toll on the body as well as the mind is a well-documented and agreed-upon conclusion of the psychiatric community".[79] The weakness becomes more visible after the traumatic experience to the point that some individuals can experience post-traumatic stress disorder. Such an emotional condition "disrupts the functioning of those afflicted by it [PTSD], interfering with their ability to meet daily needs and perform the most basic tasks".[80] That's weakness for you!

Powerlessness also emerges when a family member is belittled and put down by another family member. They feel small and lack the inner will-power to rise, thus becoming discouraged for a while. We are weakened by situations such as poverty, failure in achieving a goal or by the occurrence of a natural disaster. All of us may be weakened by injustice, unexpected disappointment or harsh oppression. In fact, more often than not, we experience emotional weakness in this life. When we are marginalised, put on the sidelines, left in the background, ostracised, or rejected, we become feeble. People in various parts of our community, society and the globe are weakened on a daily basis. Let's be honest, we all have become powerless because of some situation in our lives. When we are weakened, our energy: emotional, physical and spiritual, are sapped, drained, eroded or dried up. It can even be worse than what we have alluded to already, because some individuals never recover from that weakening event.

We are aware that the girls and their mother have been weakened by emotional issues, physical illness and marital problems. But let us ponder on how the youth will benefit from this trip. Will they be embattled with the debate on conducting healing services in private or public as some of the youth had been discussing? Will the experience at this prayer conference discourage them to the point that they become weak? Will they be forced to boycott the sessions because of theological disagreements? In particular, will Patricia benefit from this trip?

It was the last weekend in April 2004 when the young people prepared for what would become the most memorable trip of their lives for some time. At approximately 5:05 p.m, eleven of the youth, including my son and I, took the bus to the programme, with our luggage accounting for the vehicle being packed to capacity. The sun had already set since 4:26 p.m. Before the driver turned the keys to the white bus, we spent time passionately praying about the trip. Alex interceded powerfully for Mr. Normaton, the driver. Yolanda prayed inspiringly for the other drivers on the motorway and I prayed desperately that God would keep us from dangers. By the time we had set off, outside was pitched black with darkness.

The German-born George Muller, one of nineteenth-century England's immigrants, was notable for being an evangelist, missionary and director of orphanages. Prior to engaging in this noble, Muller relates that "In November I went on a pleasure trip where I spent six days in sin. My father discovered my absence before I returned, so I took all the money I could find and went to Brunswick. After spending a week at Brunswick in an expensive hotel, my money was gone. I then went, without money, to another hotel for a week. At last, the owner of the hotel, suspecting that I had no money, asked for payment and took my best clothes as security.

I walked about six miles to an inn and began to live as if I had plenty of money. On the third morning, I went quietly out of the yard and ran off. By this time the innkeeper became suspicious and had me arrested. The police questioned me for about three hours and sent me to jail. At age sixteen I became an inmate of a prison, dwelling with thieves and murderers.

After a year, the commissioner who had tried my case told my father of my conduct. I was kept in prison until he sent the money for my travelling [sic] expenses, my debt to the inn, and my stay in prison. My father arrived two days later, beat me severely, and took me home to Schoenebeck. Through more lying and persuading, I convinced him to allow me to enter school at Nordhausen the following autumn."[81]

What trip have you been on lately? What disappointment have you experienced on your journey? Did you feel as if you had had your share of disappointments? This could very well be the views of Sandra's family. As I returned to the bus ride, we had a smooth drive along the motorway. On driving into the castle yard, we heard vibrant singing emerging from a hall. We all prayerfully thanked Yahweh, the Divine One, for giving us a safe trip, jumped out and dashed for the door of the hall. We eased in and sat as discreetly as we could. I scanned the room like a lookout in search of a missing person. The ceiling was very high. Actually the hall was a two-storey-building, with various spare rooms upstairs. The back wall displayed a mural professionally painted and conveying a message. Surrounding us was a sea of young people who were riveted to their seats while the speaker preached with life and power. And there in the left hand corner, the saxophonist and the keyboard player held their spaces tightly. We were in time for the sermon, the American guest speaker's appeal, his eye-watering prayer and the final song.

After the service, we returned to the bus to collect our luggage. The youth nodded their heads in anticipation of a greater experience based on the spirit that prevailed so far.

"Wow! These are a lot of young people," Yolanda exclaimed.

"Good!" replied Julian.

Patricia, with a smile on her face, inserted:

"That preacher is great."

It was only the first session of the four-day programme. And these young people were mesmerised. Hooked. Captivated. Spellbound. They passionately yearned for the morning to arrive so that they could hear the guest speaker again. And, so that they could lead the worship session. Knowing that the young people would be attending, the programme co-ordinator had asked if our youth group could lead the worship session for one of the mornings.

It was written on their faces. This first session had brought bright emotions to their hearts. Joy. Peace. Happiness. Tranquillity. And although Patricia was beginning to tire, she too was beaming with delight.

"Coming here, showed me that there are young people still passionate for Jesus," Alex shared.

"So you think they don't have problems too?" Patricia reminded everyone.

Life seemed to have changed for them in a few short hours. Their outlook on life, their worldview of their denominational church, their perspective on the dreariness of national youth programmes had all taken a paradigm shift from that night. Within their hearts were prepared to become more focused and be more involved in the life of their local congregation. This trip certainly turned the tide for each of these young people, at least up to this point. Soon after, we took our luggage to the rooms that were allocated to us. By the time we had unpacked and settled, it was bedtime. Actually, the 'watchman' came around just after 11 p.m, announcing "lights out, please".

Just as soon as we had put our heads on the pillow, we heard loud screams coming from along the corridors. Having not fully gone to sleep, I jumped up and pushed my head out of the door. A tall guy was sprinting briskly towards my room. I inquired:

"What's going on?"

"It's someone called Patricia. She just collapsed and I am going for Pastor," he informed me.

I was between two minds about going over to her room. I approached the bathroom in my ensuite room and washed my face. With my door partly opened, I overheard someone on the corridor saying that she had recovered. With Patricia's Tinnitus is affecting her, would the fainting prevail? What could have caused this sudden fainting? Was she overburdened? Stressed? Physically? Or was there a biological issue affecting her?

Being on a journey: emotional, physical or spiritual saps our energy. It is asking for a lot. We are expected to draw on available resources. And while on our journey, we must quickly become aware that we are not the only ones taking life's journey. So we need to ask ourselves some poignant questions: Am I drifting along life's journey? What's my goal? What have I been focusing on during my journey- feeling good, a career, getting the spotlight, the welfare of others? How do I respond or react in times of weakness? Am I drawing on suitable resources or depending on my intelligence and wit? Am I a model or an example to others?

**Thoughts for Action** *[Jot down your responses]*

- What trip/journey have you been taking lately?

- Was it emotional, physical or spiritual?

- Where has that trip taken you?

**Moments of Surrender**

- As you reflect on your recent trip/journey, what have you learnt from it?

- How did you benefit from the trip which you took or are taking?

- Take this opportunity to share a powerful moment of your journey. (*Feel free to write it*).

# 10

# The Intruder

---

Approximately ten years ago, I was pursuing a postgraduate degree in Special Needs Education at a prestigious university in a Yorkshire city, in the North of England. The course entailed tedious reading and of course the assignments, educational trips and tutorials. In an effort to catch up on my course reading, I locked myself in my room. Well, I didn't need to take this precautionary measure because by this time I was alone, as far as I could tell. Well, at least there were no disturbing footsteps or slamming of doors, even though there were four other students living in this apartment: a Canadian, a Ghanaian, a Chinese and a Russian. After sitting at my varnish-coated study desk for almost an hour, I felt the need for a new environment to conduct my reading. My brightly painted room, the first on the corridor in my apartment, felt warm and gave off a stuffy odour from the ultra-marine carpet. The recently bought books heavily weighed down the bookshelves and with space being a luxury, I had to find a home for many more books, thus using a corner of the room.

I jumped up and packed my black sturdy canvas bag. Then I loaded a library book, some pens, a highlighter, my folder with all of my course notes for the semester and the research material that I had done for my upcoming thesis into it. After tidying my bed, I placed the bag in the middle of the bed and went to the kitchen to make a sandwich. While in the kitchen I became engrossed with a Western movie. By this time, I had taken a canned juice and was eating one of the sandwiches while my eyes were glued to the television. Surprisingly, Adriel, the Canadian student, pushed the kitchen door and energetically pulled up a chair to join me. Glancing at my watch, I realised that I had spent some fifteen minutes at the table. I sprang to my feet and pulling open the kitchen door, I said, "Oops! I've got to go."

As I pushed open the door of my room, I realised that my bed was empty. "Huh!" I uttered. The black bag had vanished. I was convinced that I had left it in the centre of the bed. I frantically looked behind the bed, underneath the bed and even behind my study desk. *Where could that bag be?* I thought. I dragged opened the wardrobe door and pulled out every piece of clothing. After all of that, there was no bag.

"Knock! Knock!" I rattled on Adriel's bedroom door.

"I can't find my bag. Have you seen it?"

"No. Where did you leave it?" he asked, making his way to my room.

We ripped back the six-foot mahogany wardrobe and peered behind it. Then we pulled out every piece of clothing, shook them and searched even the empty wardrobe. We still came up empty-handed. My heart sank. There was nowhere in the room to look. *Underneath the flattened carpet?* We had walked and trampled this bright blue flowered carpet countless times. It couldn't be there.[82] Someone intruded my world. It was my space, my belongings and my privacy that were violated. And life was never the same, at least not for a while. After such experiences, we keep looking over our shoulders, we become space conscious when people get too close to us, and we become more cautious, thinking that it will re-occur. Such are the consequences of an intrusion.

Back at the weekend programme, before we could put our heads on our pillows properly, it was time to rise. We woke up at 7 a.m to attend the devotional service in the hall. In spite of Patricia's difficulties with Tinnitus, she managed to sit through parts of the devotional session. However, on one occasion, the sound was too much for her and she had to leave for a short while. The worship session was inspiring, the singing lively and animated and the thought-provoking sermonette left a number of individuals in tears. Immediately after the service, the programme co-ordinator announced that there will be a special anointing service on Sunday afternoon, along with an agape feast. I wondered how some of our youth would handle the varying views among, given the fact that Patricia was expecting to experience release from her depressing situation.

On our way to breakfast, I had a short discussion with Pastor, the guest speaker.

"Pastor, is there any biblical direction on doing anointing services in public?" I asked.

"Is there a problem with the service for tomorrow?"

"What about the text in the Epistle of James which says that a sick person should extend an invitation?" I queried.

"Did sick people in the bible always invite Jesus or His disciples to heal them?" he asked.

"Not really. But what about the text in the book of James?" I pushed.

"You want to have a look at it later and then let's discuss it," the guest speaker replied as he lifted a plate from the plate-rack for his breakfast.

During breakfast, I thought seriously about his comments. I foresaw that this was a sensitive topic already. Something was brewing. *Will other young people raise their views? What will I do if other young people ask me about this provocative issue?*

Turning to the Scriptures, a survey of the healing episodes with the apostles reveals that some individuals called for healings while others did not initiate the call. As an illustration of this perspective, Scripture records that, after biblical characters, Ananias and his wife Sapphira dropped dead, on agreeing to cheat by keeping back part of the funds they received after selling a plot of land, "great fear came upon all the church and upon all who heard these things" (Acts 5:11). This event was a manifestation of divine power through the apostles, to the point where many people accepted the apostles' message and joined the church.

With there being many believers of all walks of life among the community of believers at that time, individuals who knew of sick and ailing people, brought them to receive healing (Acts 5:15). This act enabled sick individuals to experience healing in such a dynamic setting. Luke, the author of Acts of the Apostles, reports that there were so many people present that the believers laid the people everywhere, so that even the Apostle Peter's shadow could heal them (v.15b).[83] Luke's account implies that these individuals called for divine healing in that they brought the sick to the disciples, thus indicating that the people summoned or invited the leaders of the church to conduct the healing publicly among the huge crowd that was present (v.16). In fact, Michael Perham argues that "The ministry of healing has its proper place in the public liturgy of the Church [sic]. Where it happens in home or hospital, that is an extension of a ministry that is corporate and public."[84] So even though the author of this biblical account does not indicate the method used in the healing, we are cognisant of the apostles engaging in divine healing which was witnessed by numerous people.

Returning to the events in the eating area, as soon as breakfast was finished, a few young men gathered around a table that was positioned unobtrusively in a corner of the dining area. Alex, Sophia and I had joined in the discussion. One of the other young men opened the discussion:

"The book of James tells us that the sick should call the church elders to themselves."

"But what if people are really sick and don't know or can't even think about those things' Alex asked.

"We have to be careful that we are not putting our own view on the issue," I enforced.

At the same time, the programme director passed by. On overhearing the discussion, he firmly warned the guys. I nudged one of the guys and he backed down.

Immediately, we rushed off to our rooms to collect our books in preparation for the first group bible study. As she briskly walked along the corridor to her room, Patricia reflected,

*"I don't know what all the fuss is about. Some people don't know how a situation feels until they are in it. All this confusion is foolishness."*

When we really think about it, this issue is really about executing the anointing as opposed to the doctrine or contents of such as service. Michael Perham in observing that the Church has been given the gift of healing, advocates that "... the ministry of healing should form part of the regular liturgical life of each community. Whether on a weekly, monthly or quarterly basis, there needs to be an occasion when this ministry is offered and seen to be very much at the heart of the Church's sacramental life."[85] Is this view calling for anointing to take place in the worship service often? This seems to be the case, but does this mean that anointing should be conducted like the communion service? Certainly not, but the congregation needs to know that healing is available, whereby, not only the physical ill, but the hurting, troubled or perplexed congregants can be made whole.

Later that day, we attended the mid-day service. Patricia and Sophia were sitting together. During the worship session, which a team of young people were leading, Patricia slumped to the ground. There were screams and great commotion. Everyone was stunned. A few people were asking: "What's wrong?" "Is she hurt?" Someone took a fan to cool her, seeing that she was perspiring like the lid of a boiling pot. It was only a few minutes, but during that time, everything had stopped. The young people were huddled together, praying fervently for Patricia. Certainly, her situation indicated the need for prayer and even an anointing. She was collapsing frequently. Should an invitation be given for the pastor to pray and anoint those who are sick?

Take a step back for a moment. Does it really matter if we invite a church leader to perform an anointing service or not? What would you have done if your children needed relief from a physical or emotional ailment? Were these young people insensitive to those individuals who needed healing? Would you have allowed yourself to be anointed, after travelling approximately two hundred miles, only to discover that some element of a church service was not conducted according to biblical guidelines?

In Acts 3:1-8, we read that "One day Peter and John were going up to the temple at the time of prayer—at three in the afternoon. Now a man crippled from birth was being carried to the temple gate called Beautiful, where he was put every day to beg from those going into the temple courts. When he saw Peter and John about to enter, he asked them for money. Peter looked straight at him, as did John. Then Peter said, 'Look at us!' So the man gave them his attention, expecting to get something from them. Then Peter said, 'Silver or gold I do not have, but what I have I give you. In the name of Jesus Christ of Nazareth, walk.' Taking him by the right hand, he helped him up, and instantly the man's feet and ankles became strong. He jumped to his feet and began to walk. Then he went with them into the temple courts, walking and jumping, and praising God" (NIV). This episode identifies a man who was habitually placed at the temple gate, where he earned his daily living by begging. There is no indication that he sent or directly asked these two apostles for healing. And although "characters in Acts [of the Apostles] practice [sic] almsgiving, Peter and John sidestep this responsibility, for the focus in this account is to be on their exercise of divine power."[86]

As we cast our minds back to events at the castle, everyone had had a two-hour rest period after lunch. About an hour into the rest period, Yolanda, Sophia and a few other females huddled around Patricia in the yard. They had congregated in outside underneath a tree, while sitting on a dark-stained bench. It was a bright day, with the sunshine beaming from the heavens. The atmosphere was placid. Not even the birds were visible. The pink roses in the garden glittered and bloomed in the brilliant sunlight. The gravel underneath the girls' feet made a scrunching sound. It was hardly music to the ear. There on the bench, the girls hugged and chatted with each other. Patricia's community had to come to her rescue. They supported her with their presence and prayers. Such acts of kindness are therapeutic for the hurting and the weak and have an impact on the speed at which such individuals experience healing.

Let's go back to the Scripture for a moment. A similar healing took place in Acts 9 where we read that "there was in Damascus a disciple named Ananias.... And the Lord said to him, 'Get up and go to the street called Straight and ask at the house of Judas for a man of Tarsus named Saul, for behold, he is praying [there]. And he has seen in a vision a man named Ananias, enter and lay his hands on him so that he might regain his sight.' So Ananias left and went into the house. And he laid his hands on Saul and said, 'Brother Saul, the Lord Jesus, Who appeared to you along the way by which you came here, has sent me that you may recover your sight and be filled with the Holy Spirit.' And instantly something like scales fell from [Saul's] eyes, and he recovered his sight. Then he arose and was baptized" (vv 10, 11, 17 and 18, AMP). Here, Paul, having being blinded by a bright heavenly light, did not request healing, but God, in demonstrating His love and care, instructed Ananias to heal the visually-impaired Paul. Does God contradict Himself? Does the bible oppose itself? Does the practice of Jesus' disciples contradict the biblical principles provided through the inspiration of the Holy Spirit? These episodes appear to demonstrate God's concern with bringing relief to the hurting and the suffering as opposed to following rules and regulations. It is true that God does not intrude or impose His will on us, but because He reads and detects the heart's motives, such acts of healing are beyond an invitational-uninvitational debate.

There is a further consideration. God's demonstration of divine power through His Apostles in the Early Church indicates a perpetuation of Jesus' ministry, even though He has returned to Heaven. In reflecting on Jesus' earthly ministry, we notice that "During His life on earth, the sick and afflicted were objects of His special compassion. When He sent out His disciples, He commissioned them to heal the sick as well as to preach the gospel. When He sent forth the seventy, He commanded them to heal the sick, and next to preach that the kingdom of God had come nigh unto them. Their physical health was to be first cared for, in order that the way might be prepared for the truth to reach their minds. The Saviour devoted more time and labor to healing the afflicted of their maladies than to preaching. His last injunction to His apostles, His representatives on earth, was to lay hands on the sick that they might recover. When the Master shall come, He will commend those who have visited the sick and relieved the necessities of the afflicted."[87] Having this perspective of Jesus and His involvement in ministry allows us to move beyond the narrow issue of extending or not extending an invitation to church leaders to conduct a healing service.

We are also aware that "Christ has empowered His church to do the same work that He did during His ministry. Today He is the same compassionate physician that He was while on this earth. We should let the afflicted understand that in Him there is healing balm for every disease, restoring power for every infirmity. His disciples in this time are to pray for the sick as verily as His disciples of old prayed."[88] Such views highlight the extent of the church's responsibility in contemporary times when hurting families are in needs of healing, be it emotional, physical or spiritual. Moreover, Kate Litchfield explains that Christian pastoral care tends to be messy because pastoral care-givers attempt to get "closer to the messy reality of people's lives, where they share their troubles." [89] With this being the case she upholds the spontaneity of various forms of Christian pastoral care and indicates that a minister may initiate the provision of such forms of pastoral care.[90] From this, can we conclude that an invitation is not always necessary for providing pastoral care, whether it be conducting divine healing, prayer or providing spiritual guidance?

Reverting to the meeting the girls and Patricia, Yolanda tried to encourage the weakened Patricia to take part in the anointing service and agape feast.

"I heard the discussion some of you were having earlier," Yolanda alerted Patricia.

"What discussion?" Patricia asked.

"About the anointing."

"Everybody has a view. Why do we have to make things so complicated?" She asked.

"I think you should focus on getting better," Sophia chipped in at this moment.

"You're right. It's just that I am confused by all this fuss," Patricia confessed.

The girls stood to return to their room to join some of the others, when Alex rushed through the main door. A trail of other young people followed him.

"What's wrong?" the leader queried.

"Apparently Julian got a group of boys together to discuss the issue about the anointing service tomorrow and the word got around that they are planning to boycott it. We heard that people were told to join in the boycott and the co-ordinator heard about it," Alex informed us, looking agitated.

"Where is Jane?" her sister, Yolanda asked.

People who intrude on your space causes you to avoid them like the plague. Actually, it's more like boycott, where we refuse commercial, social or political relations with either a product, person, group, store, church, organisation or country. Engaging in a boycott occurs at the request of someone or based on personal choice. To boycott something means not only depriving those we are boycotting, but also depriving ourselves of something we would have otherwise used or taken advantage of under normal circumstances. In any case, we disassociate ourselves, pass by or shun the target. It's about refusing to purchase, attend, support, travel to the object of our actions.

We engage in boycotts because somebody has messed up and the behaviour has touched our moral nerve. The perpetrator's behaviour elicits red hot anger and irritation that were boiling with us. For instance, take the call to boycott a popular American weekly magazine which is distributed to mainland America and other international countries. The reason? The creator of a musical comedy-drama television series aired on one of America's television channels became furious about an alleged homophobic article that was circulated in this weekly magazine. His goal is a complete and immediate boycott of the magazine until an apology is sent to the victim in the article.

Turning your attention back to the conversation in the castle's yard, Yolanda waited impatiently for a response about her sister.

"It looks as though she was in the 'gang' and pastor is looking for this 'gang'. I heard that he may send home the 'gang' leaders unless they apologise," Alex added.

"Let me find my young people," our leader announced.

Sophia rushed off. On checking for everyone, she discovered that they were all in their rooms. Boys and girls. Apparently, the threat to send someone home had frightened everyone. They were on their 'Ps and Qs'. The rest of the afternoon was spent focusing on the scheduled activities. Everyone was feeling the pressure because of the packed day's programme. They had attended intensive bible study sessions, prayer sessions, two worship services, special meetings with their groups and also tried to socialise with young people from other churches.

Let's face it. All of us have our own views on this sensitive subject. But where do you stand on the topic? Have you also aired you views in the past? Were you one of those individuals who refuse to be flexible? Do you follow the letter of the Scriptures or operate in the spirit to aid the weak and hurting? Do you see conducting an anointing service which was not requested by those who are hurting as an intrusion?

## Thoughts for Action *[Jot down your responses]*

- Has someone ever intruded your space or property? What was your reaction?

- Would you be willing to take any form of Christian pastoral care such as prayer, an anointing or pastoral visit, even though you have not requested it?

- Is there a life-threatening ailment for which you desire healing?

- To whom are you planning to go to acquire the healing: Doctor, psychotherapist, pastor or family therapist?

- How does this chapter help you in your pursuit of deliverance from that ailment?

**Moments of Surrender**

- Take some time to contemplate on your decision to obtain healing. Spend some time preparing for the healing occasion

# 11

# Private-Keep Out!

Private: Keep Out!- is a popular sign used to warn intruders to keep off some one's property. It could be a personal journal, a bedroom, a study, an office, a driveway, a road, a house, or a plot of land. These useful cautionary signs can come in different dimensions, be it 40 cm x 30 cm or 60 cm x 40 cm. The manufacturers are willing to provide different types of materials such as: stoved aluminium, rigid plastic, self adhesive vinyl and polycarbonate, from which customers can choose. These specifications temptingly lure customers into making selections from a variety of choices by which they can meet their needs.

On Sunday morning, after everyone had attended the devotion service and completed breakfast, individuals rushed into their respective study groups for bible studies. Some of the youth seemed to have absconded and deserted the Sunday morning sessions. In fact, many of them could hardly rise early because they were up until late Saturday night. It was customary every year to allow the youth to engage in playing a melody of songs and hymns each Saturday night after the main programme. This particular year was no different. This time of inspiring praise and worship lasted until 12 midnight. The owners of the compound had imposed that cut-off time on us. With adrenalin still high after this vibrant session, some of the youth set up a six-side football game under the moonlight in the yard. Others were socialising and chatting heartily with new-found friends.

There was no rush to retire early. It was Saturday night-time for socialising, becoming acquainted and just 'letting one's hair down'.

Halfway into the studies, the programme co-ordinator circled the compound checking on the attendance. Nevertheless, with an understanding heart, he ignored it and encouraged the group leaders to conduct the study sessions speedily. In a few minutes, other groups were trickling out of their respective rooms, indicating that they were finished. Meanwhile, the pastor stood at the entrance of the hall. It was unusual. *Was he there to do a head count? Was he spying on us? Or was he looking for the 'gang' leader?* Sure enough, Julian approached the door. The Pastor pulled him aside and had an animated discussion with him. He gesticulated with his hands. Julian's head was bowed. Whatever they were discussing put this young male youth in a humbling position. The heat seemed to have cooled. Afterwards they entered the hall. By then everyone had gathered in the main hall, where instructions were given about the procedure and time for the agape feast and the anointing service. By this time, dinner was ready.

Let's ponder on the idea of desertion for a moment! Desertion in life occurs when individuals believe that an activity is too emotionally demanding and psychologically absorbing. They are unable to cope emotionally and thus, become affected physically. We are unable to rise to the challenge. To produce. To contribute. Have you been there? Who have you deserted? What have you deserted? That funeral of a dear friend because both of you clashed a few years ago? A birthday party of your work colleague because you were notified at the last minute? The wedding of a family member-mother, father or sister, because you didn't approve of the spouse-to-be? Emerging from the shadows of desertion is never easy. Too many questions to be answered. Too many people to whom you are accountable. And too much ground to cover.

With the plates clattering and the cutlery making tinkling noise in the dining area at the castle, Patricia asked:

"Shouldn't the pastor do the anointing privately?"

"What do you mean?" I opened.

"Do you know anything about healing?" she asked me.

"Let me get back to you," I replied.

Think about it. The Holy Scriptures record examples of miracles conducted in private, one of which is found in Acts 9: "There was a believer in Joppa named Tabitha (which in Greek is Dorcas). She was always doing kind things for others and helping the poor. About this time she became ill and died. Her body was washed for burial and laid in an upstairs room. But the believers had heard that Peter was nearby at Lydda, so they sent two men to beg him, 'Please come as soon as possible!' So Peter returned with them; and as soon as he arrived, they took him to the upstairs room. The room was filled with widows who were weeping and showing him the coats and other clothes Dorcas had made for them. But Peter asked them all to leave the room; then he knelt and prayed. Turning to the body he said, 'Get up, Tabitha.' And she opened her eyes! When she saw Peter, she sat up! He gave her his hand and helped her up. Then he called in the widows and all the believers, and he presented her to them alive. The news spread through the whole town, and many believed in the Lord" (vv 36-42, NLT). Behind the private walls of that upper room, the miracle that occurs is an "acknowledgement that God is act work."[91] But what could have instigated Peter to oust the widows and the mourners from the room where the dead woman lay? Absence of faith among them? Following Jesus' example? Could it be that the crying and bawling were signs of distrust in Divine power, seeing that they had already sent for the Apostle? Or did he desire to have an intimate moment with God before engaging in the miraculous event?

Moreover, Scripture highlights the performance of a few other miracles in a private place, actions which could be in support of James 5:13-16, where the sick are instructed to call the elders to him/herself. Acts 28 records another instance of healing done privately: "Near the shore where we landed was an estate belonging to Publius, the chief official of the island. He welcomed us and treated us kindly for three days. As it happened, Publius's father was ill with fever and dysentery. Paul went in and prayed for him, and laying his hands on him, he healed him. Then all the other sick people on the island came and were healed. As a result we were showered with honors, and when the time came to sail, people supplied us with everything we would need for the trip" (vv. 7-10, NLT). Here the clause 'went in and prayed for him, and laying his hands on him' seems incompatible to the imperative: 'Let him call for the elders of the church, and let them pray over him, anointing him with oil'. In fact we already established that the Greek translation of *proskaleomai,* a verb in the middle voice, indicates that the sick individual should summon or invite the church leaders to him/herself. Although Paul conducted the healing in a room, does James' statement mean that the sick should invite church leaders to a special room, the pastor's office, the main worship hall or to the sick person's home?

As Christian believers, we should let reason prevail and avoid any practices that would misguide the non-believers. It is true, as Dow and Stammers rightly contend, that "Some forms of Christian ministry in which healing is prominent are wide open to the charge of sensationalism. Those doing this ministry would reply that when Jesus was doing His ministry with integrity the results were so astonishing that reports about it spread very rapidly. The problem seems to be that some present-day members of the clergy appear deliberately to play up the supposed miraculous nature of the cures. However, there is no evidence of Jesus doing this, rather the opposite."[92] It may, therefore, be expedient and more appropriate to refrain from public divine healing, if only to avoid a spectacle and also to prevent this sacred rite from being exploited.

Returning to the discussion with Patricia, we finished our dinner. Then I beckoned to Patricia that I needed to have a chat with her. Everyone, but the kitchen staff left us at the dinner tables. Patricia was fainting too frequently. I felt I needed to find the cause. It certainly wasn't a physical problem. With my psychological background, I spoke with her:

"I want you to share with me what goes through your mind just before you faint."

"What do you mean?" she queried innocently.

"What do you find yourself thinking about?"

"A friend," she shared.

"Anything in particular about the friend?" I asked.

"A friend whom I like a lot."

"What do you mean?"

"I fancy the person," she explained.

"I take it this is your fiancé," I added.

"Yep. My mum disagrees with it. And I feel she is annoyed at me for running away."

In that instant, she broke down in tears. My heart reached out to her. Clearly, she was in turmoil. There seemed to be emotional pain, emotional burdens and emotional pressure bearing down on her. This one was beyond me. I perceived that she needed counselling from a professional practitioner. A psychotherapist would reach her better. Could it be that guilt was plaguing her mind? Could it be that at her age, she was not equipped emotionally for an intimate relationship? I spent some time praying with her and encouraged her to attend the anointing service.

She wiped her tears away and then we left. As we sauntered along the corridors, Patricia admitted:

"I am really enjoying the sessions, but I don't know about tomorrow's service."

"What is your heart telling?" I asked..

"I want to do it, but..." Patricia contended.

Fatigue was telling on our bodies. She yawned, as a sign of fatigue. Having gone to my room, I dived into my bunk bed and was soon knocked out with exhaustion. I didn't seem as if I had slept for long when I heard a deafening alarm.

When we focus on the subject of healing it can be a contentious one. Although Dow and Stammers contend that we should be cautious in conducting divine healing publicly, they, on the other hand, argue that "It seems entirely appropriate to pray for personal healing when the Church meets for worship."[93] Does this mean we should make an appeal for anyone who is sick to approach the altar for special prayer during the main service, when the pastoral prayer is given? Does the view of Dow and Stammers include all types of sickness? Is there a need for the recipient and the pray-er to be prepared themselves for this special service in advance? Does repentance and restitution need to be carried out before hand?

The alarm which I heard was in the form of human voices. It was the two programme assistant co-ordinators who were stirring everyone. They had been given the tedious job of climbing the steep ancient castle stairs to round up all the youth in preparation for the agape feast and the anointing. I swiftly arose, got dressed and waded my way down the spiralling staircase. By the time I reached the entrance to the hall most of the young people were queued up in twos waiting to enter the 'pearly gates'.

A few minutes later, the doors were swung open and we entered. It was like the biblical character, Moses, going into God's presence when he saw the burning bush, as recorded in the book of Exodus. We were instructed to leave our shoes at the door because everyone would be sitting on the floor. The main hall was transformed. The chairs were neatly stacked away. Fruits and nuts of all kind were neatly laid out in trays. Oranges, plums, small pieces of bananas, seeded and seedless grapes were well placed in our view.

What we saw on the floor was awesome. Small red and white candles flickered brightly. They were placed in such a way that to form the shape of a cross. The scene was set. The oil was placed on a small table. The worship team was in place. The musicians were poised to provide backup. The guest speaker sat quietly waiting for the service to commence. And I looked around only to discover that some of the girls were missing. A few of the youth looked in my direction. Did the missing ones go the toilets? Did they rush back to their rooms for something? The service began with a song service. Like clockwork, two of us rose from our 'seats' and quietly exited the worship hall. We found the missing ones perched on some benches in the dining area.

"You should be in the hall. The service is about to start," the leader informed them.

"I don't feel like going," Patricia replied.

"I hear one person saying this and another saying that. I don't know what or who to believe," she breathed out.

"I thought we had come to an agreement," I confirmed.

I was dumbfounded for a while. My mind was racing speedily. *Did the young people's views poison her mind about the anointing service? Was she rebelling?* Sophia pleaded in desperation and her heart beat rapidly. A bitter and dark fear was written on Patricia's face. Her face lengthened. Her eyes popped out. She was afraid of not being healed. Fear of going back home with the same ailments. Fear of being blamed by her mother. Confusion. Panic. Uncertainty.

Then she surrendered. On returning to the main hall, the anointing service was already in progress. With all the uncertainty and chaos that prevailed, I empathised with Patricia. *Will she fly into a rage? Will she go forward and be anointed?* I Pondered deeply as I found a space between two young people.

The worship team switched to a prayerful song, while, the guest speaker, stood to his feet and took his place near the table with the oil. He extended the invitation to those who needed anointing for any ailment and as the worship team continued, a queue began to form. The melodious songs riveted our hearts, moving some of us to tears. The atmosphere became solemn almost instantly. The musicians were so engrossed in working the instruments that I detected the harmony. The music glided across my ears. It was sentimental. Melodious. Soothing. Captivating. Many of us became emotional with tears dripping from our eyes. Meanwhile, the queue had become very short. And still Patricia hadn't moved.

Back on the outside, the weather changed almost instantly with heavy showers. It seemed like a heavenly omen with prophetic significance for the ailing, afflicted, annoyed, broken, depressed and the tortured. I stared through the wide transparent glass into the yard. From what I could visualise, it appeared that the torrential downpour seemed truly sudden because even the chirping birds rushed at top speed to escape being drowned by the gushing water from the heavens.

As soon as the last person rose from his kneeling, I heard a voice from the front asking:

"Is there anyone...?"

Before Mr Hollows could complete his question, Sophia, holding Patricia's hand led her to the 'altar' to be prayed for and anointed. Various exclamations emerged from the congregation:

"Amen! Umm! Yes!"

As Mr. Hollows was about to lay his hands on Patricia's forehead, she began to weep bitterly. She screamed and wailed. Both pastors were somewhat surprisingly overtaken by the events. They gathered around her. What could have moved her to tears? Did she see herself as unworthy? A failure? Not fit to be loved? We were bewildered by Patricia's behaviour and mood.

When we are confronted with hurting families, that is not the time to debate the how and where of their cases. Families, who turn up at the doctor's surgery, pastor's office, counsellor's therapy room, are interested in one thing - finding a cure for their problem. Raising the wounded should be paramount for us, especially when we are grasping for hope in the midst of despair. Certainly, this is what healing wounds are all about- hearing and responding to the desperate pleas of weak families. No amount of philosophising or rationalising can erase this singular goal of hurting families. What level of responsibility will you extend to such families? Do you allow your personal views to prevent the needy and weak from finding relief? Is your support for your community dependent on how your views are accepted?

**Thoughts for Action** *[Jot down your responses]*

- How has the private moment you had with the General Practitioner (GP), your pastor/parish priest, or psychotherapist helped you with your personal situation?

- What personal issues did this chapter address for you?

- Identify a topic or subject on which you have unchanging views.

- How would your views impact on your responsibility towards a member of your community who are in need of help, be it emotional, physical or spiritual?

**Moments of Surrender**

- Take some time to reflect on those private thoughts and deeds that you have not shared with anyone. (You can write them out)

- Have you shared them in prayer? Are you willing to do so at this moment?

# 12

# A Touch of Care

Therapist, Lena Canada, engineers a novel treatment in working with Karen, a cerebral palsy patient, who is wheelchair-bound. As Karen pathetically struggles with the medical condition which is causing her life to ebb away slowly, she elicits joy and fulfilment from a therapeutic treatment, that of exchanging letters with rock singer, Elvis Presley. However, the more the physically disabled Karen receives encouraging and emotionally uplifting letters and gifts from Elvis, the more the affectionate bond is transformed into an incredible influence over her. Yet, the horrendous physical disability gradually contributed to her grotesque, horrifying and skinny body decaying. In the end, Karen's death gripped Lena with severe grief. On a number of occasions while driving near Elvis' home, Lena hallucinated and envisaged Elvis smiling at her. Such is the deep impact of a patient's death on its therapist.

Sony Pictures' classic *Touched by Love* is a 95-minute emotionally dramatic film, which has induced nostalgic feeling in millions of Americans. This double award-nominated film attracted thousands of fans who were fascinated by actress Diane Lane and singer Elvis Presley. The 1980 movie was inspired by Lena Canada's out-of-print book, *To Elvis, with Love* and is a portrayal of love, hope and devotion, which we all dream to have. It's an emotionally charged movie in which everyone is touched- touched by the pain, and equally by the compassion that Lena and Elvis displayed.

Reflecting on Patricia's ordeal and the help that she attracted, we can conclude that she too was *Touched by Love*. However, it goes beyond love, it is *a touch of care*. Back in the main hall at the castle, a few of us had surrounded Patricia and passionately interceded for her in Christ's Name, while everyone else sang solemnly and prayerfully. Her painful tears eventually subsided. But she was perspiring profusely.

By the way, whenever we are faced with our grief, illness or some other disturbing health issue, there is a longing for an instant and urgent remedy. But we seldom see the importance of the various spiritual activities that take place in the context of pastoral ministry. That is why we could agree with Steven Croft, who reminds us that: "At the heart of pastoral ministry is a desire to bring the grace of God lovingly and sensitively into the lives of men and women and children, often in times of great need. This will involve, often, not only prayer for people through intercession but prayer with people, often involving laying on of hands or anointing for strength and for healing in different contexts."[94]

The guest speaker spoke with Patricia:

"What is your name,"

"Patricia."

"What are you feeling, Patricia?" he inquired.

"I don't like what I did."

"What do you mean?" the pastor probed further.

"My parents are mad at me for running away."

"What made you run away?"

"There were too many problems at home."

"Would you like to talk to the Lord about it?" he suggested.

"I want to. It's on my mind all the time."

It was guilt. Ever since that evening when Samuel slapped Patricia, she had been carrying the anger. She wanted to be independent. Be away from her protective parents. She felt that running away was the answer. Although she mentally craved for it, her conscience spoke with conviction that evening. The guilt had surfaced and gripped her like an octopus and a ferocious pitbull dog. It had gnawed at her thoughts and tore the layers of anger away. It awoke the bitterness she carried in her heart for her parents. Guilt can be destructive, malignant and poisonous. It spreads to the mind, the body, the heart and the soul. It penetrates the thoughts with poisonous beliefs, distorted views and leads to a display of undesirable behaviours. The short exchange between Patricia and the guest speaker corroborates Christian psychologist, Gary R. Collins' view that "Sometimes counselees respond to confrontation with confession and a significant experience of forgiveness. Often, however, confrontation brings resistance, guilt, hurt, or anger."[95]

Various relationship-destroying situations emerge as a result of guilt feelings. For example, guilt creates a platform for human suffering to the extent that "people who are depressed, lonely, grieving, members of a violent family... experience guilt as part of their difficulties."[96] Individuals who are riddled with guilt tend to display violent behaviours, which then have a negative impact on other people. Consequently, poor inter-relationships become the product of guilt, thus preventing us from experiencing the healing that we need or from responding to the desperate call of the weak. A disrupted relationship with an individual often blurs our relationship with God, thus causing us to question our religious faith in Him.

Another impact is that our psychological development becomes stifled because of the subjective guilt which we carry. Collins describes subjective guilt as "an uncomfortable feeling of regret, remorse, shame and self-condemnation that often comes when we have done or thought something that we feel is wrong." [97] In particular, areas such as self esteem and a sense of intimacy are affected negatively, thus producing a low self esteem and a sense of isolation. As a result, individuals who fail to form meaningful personal relationships with others tend to experience failure in loving people.[98] So when we consider the harsh reality we experience because of guilt feelings, we see the importance of having an opportunity to release our guilt.

The soothing, solemn singing in the main hall had subsided, but the musicians continued. Patricia was beaming in her face. Her tender eyes appeared calm. Soon after, the service climaxed, on a pinnacle, with the final song. Immediately, everyone headed to his/her room. The solemnity of the service compelled the youth to be reverend for the remainder of the evening. It was as if a heavenly halo overshadowed everyone due to fact that we all retired early for the night. But, on realising that Patricia was absorbing the heart-and life-changing experiences, I wondered how she would be able to maintain this transformation on returning home. And you are probably wondering like myself what would happen to this changed girl who had found some degree of happiness for once.

It was heart-warming and encouraging to witness her experiencing a touch of care. Kate Litchfield advocates that "Pastoral care is rooted in prayer to God since He is the only person that can restore us holistically. Indeed it is not the power of the care-giver that brings about any changes, but by the power of God, to whom we lift the wounded." [99] Nothing can be more soothing and comforting to a wounded family than to know that someone has been praying tirelessly for its members. And the changes that a family experiences occur because of the grace of God and His omnipotence in working on their behalf.

It was 7:10 a.m when an alarm went off. By this time some individuals were in the bathroom, a few were still snoring heavily, a few were already down stairs with their luggage, while one or two loitered indolently and aimlessly on the elongated narrow corridor chatting with each other. I poked my head out of my bedroom's door, only to discover that it was the human voices of the assistant programme co-ordinators warning us that we had to take all our luggage out by 10 a.m and that we could not returned.

By 1:00 p.m the programme had ended. We packed our luggage in the bus, painfully greeted our new-found friends and took photos as souvenirs. Mobile phones, digital cameras, simple flash cameras. Every type of photo-taking equipment that could be used was employed to catch the last-minute memories of an inspirational and emotional prayer conference. People were waving goodbyes, even as the buses, cars and vans were crawling out through the gate at a cautionary speed of 5 miles per hour. As our bus picked up speed, the sight of the castle faded away gradually. As the bus picked up momentum, I began thinking: *Who could I approach to help Patricia? Would she be able to fit back into her home?* These thought flooded my mind for a while. But then I snapped out of my reflective mood and began chatting with the other passengers.

Individuals, who experience Christian pastoral care, be it in the form of counselling, prayer or visitation, perceive the leaders as being interested in their well-being. But when we provide pastoral care, we help the receiver interpret their experiences and make sense of their lives. Perham reminds us that "the local church needs to appreciate, teach and practice the ministry of healing." [100] And when we reflect on the importance of pastoral care, we would agree that divine healing, as a form of pastoral care should not be done in a vacuum, but should be accompanied by counselling, reflection and sharing by the recipient and a follow up visit or call.[101]

During a hectic day, an anonymous woman joined in a crowd which followed Jesus and his disciples, who were making their way to restore a Jewish ruler's dead daughter. The dust ascended into the atmosphere. Clothing flapped in the strong breeze which rushed across Nazareth. This weak and desperate lady had had a severe bout of haemorrhaging for approximately twelve years and although she travelled far and wide to find a cure and the best treatment, not even the best medical teams of her day could provide a remedy for this life-threatening illness.

Having glimpsed Jesus in the crowd, she braced herself and made a last ditch-effort to attempt to be healed. This was a rare occasion since Jesus hardly passed through a city or town on more than one or two occasions. Everyone was chatting. The Jewish ruler and Jesus were engaged in a deep conversation, perhaps sharing some of the bitter and difficult moments of his daughter's life. The ailing woman, although weakened by her illness, was energised by the sight of Jesus and the thought of being healed. She pushed through the frantic crowd and without recognising it, she was at arm's length from him. Without much pomp and style, she reached down and touched the edge of his clothing.

Something must have stirred Jesus inwardly and spiritually, because he became aware that something special had happened to Him even though the crowd surrounded Him. He looked around to see if He could perceive a changed human being. Well, this woman could not hide. She felt the need to share her story. Stepping forward, she bowed in reverence and awe, looked Him in the eye and broke her silence. There must have been gasps and subdued voices of awe. The miracle worker and the Jewish Messiah turned, reached out and commended this woman for her faith. Immediately, she felt it. Healed and restored. What a touch!

Returning to Patricia's family ordeal, a few days later, Sandra called to make an appointment to see me. Within two days we had met.

"Patricia is doing a lot better, but I would like to give her more help. What can you do for her," Sandra shared.

"I believe we can ask Sharon to have some sessions with her. Don't forget that she is in the medical field and would be more able to help," I added.

"How am I going to do that?" she asked with a concerned look.

"Leave it to me. I will approach her, if you agree" I assured her.

I alerted Sandra that we would have to get Patricia's consent for her to meet with Sharon and myself.

Sometime later, I called the kind, business-like medic.

"Hi, good evening."

"Hi, how are you?" she asked.

"Fine. I need to chat with you about a situation. You know that Patricia has been fainting for a while now. Well, I had a chat with her a few weeks ago and I am convinced that there are no physical problems. I believe she is emotionally pressured. Do you think you can help?

"The only time I really have is on Sundays, and then it wouldn't be every Sunday," Sharon explained.

"Have a think and you can get back to me, later," I informed her.

"O.K. Later," Sharon replied.

Having alerted Patricia of our need to give her further support, Sharon and I had the first meeting with Sandra and Samuel. We set up one-to-one sessions with the parents and same-gender sessions. During a one-to-one session with Sandra, she opened up more:

"There is something else I need to share with you. If Patricia is to recuperate fully, I need to make a hard decision," she explained.

"What are you thinking?" I asked.

"I have been searching desperately for help for some time and I believe it has come. I have lost Janice and I can't afford to lose my other children."

"What made you feel so desperate?" I delved.

"I guess when you have been in a difficult situation for a long time, and you can't seem to get out, you panic and desperation sets in. You find yourself doing anything that would help you out of the situation," mum admitted.

"So, is that why you were checking to see what other denominations believe about healing?" I injected.

"Well, I had to do something," she confessed.

Let's pause for a moment and consider the impact of desperation. Actually, when you are desperate you engage in do-or-die behaviours, you tap into the thing or person you consider to be a last resort. You move with urgency because you sense that your hope is waning and you are powerless to stop it. You sense that time is against you and there is a fear that the clock will strike the hour before you get the assistance or deliverance for which you crave. Have you ever been desperate? Longing for something to happen in your life? Hoping to hear a positive word from the doctor, a store manager about a job or the records department about your exam results? How did you deal with your anxiety?

We continued the conversation.

"I think we need some time away from this home, so that Patricia can clear her mind. I have made up my mind," she shared boldly.

This no-nonsense mother was about to drop a bomb-shell. Would her children benefit from her next move? Is it a selfish move? Did she consider all of her options?

"I have decided to move out from the house. If I don't, Patricia will struggle again and I can't have that. This is it," mum opened up.

"How definite is your decision? So, what is going to happen to the house you have been paying for all those years? And your marriage relationship?" I pressed further.

"I haven't got there yet. I just need to get out."

*A Touch of care.* That's what this family experienced - in the form of affection, nurture, protection, and spiritual guidance. With various individuals sharing love and sympathy, this family's pent-up emotions became absorbed by the display of community responsibility. Sharing a perspective on such a display, Kate Litchfield argues that "Pastoral care is central to the life of the Church and determined by the command to love God... and one's neighbour as oneself." She further contends then that "The fundamental aim of pastoral care is the enactment of this love, incorporating the pastoral functions of healing, sustaining, guiding and reconciling."[102] The wounded, who experiences nurture from tender and caring individuals, especially if they are members of the same community, gain a certain quality of life. Although most people longingly expect relief from their ailments, they mainly appreciate the environment which provides them with happiness, hope, laughter and peace of mind. The desperate pleas of families may be calling for such elements of life, which only we can assist them in receiving.

**Thoughts for Action** *[Jot down your responses]*

- Has your life been touched by some one's care or presence?

- How have you benefited from this care or presence?

- Is there something or someone that you have been holding onto for a while in a negative way?

- Is it worth holding onto at this stage in your life?

- What steps can you take to get rid of it: ask for special prayer, attend counselling, request an anointing, or share it with a trusted friend?

**Moments of Surrender**

- Take some time to reflect on how caring your community has been over the last few weeks, months or years.

- How can you contribute to the degree of care you expect?

- What would it take for your community to improve the level of care it demonstrates at present to its members?

# 13

# Life Began at 45

Sweet sixteen is a landmark birthday for 16-year old teenagers. It's an acknowledgement that they have transitioned from childhood to adulthood. In many societies, teenagers excitingly treasure their sixteen birthday, knowing that certain extra privileges come with it. It's an important milestone because some are able to obtain their driver's licenses. Receiving the privilege to drive is often a time of great excitement for teens-all the more reason for one's 16th birthday to be more thrilling and important. In most societies, a person's 16th birthday is a very momentous occasion and is celebrated with great fanfare. A 16th birthday party is viewed by many teens as an anniversary and requires a huge celebration. As a result, the birthday celebration is often bigger and more elaborate than any other birthday. The party involves more preparations, more people and more decorations.

Soon after that memorable occasion, their 21st birthday appears. When individuals turn 21, they herald it as a definite landmark- perhaps the biggest landmark because they can participate independently in every activity that is earmarked for adults. Many individuals dream of reaching their 21st birthday because numerous rights and responsibilities await them.

A few years after having fun, hunting for jobs, settling into a career and 'catching your feet', the familiar ancient adage kicks in: life begins at forty. This seems to be the resurgence of landmarks in one's life because of the focus on this age. Forty is seen as the age of wisdom, hence insightful quotes are generated. Take for example the French proverb: forty is the old age of youth; fifty is the youth of old age. Or the quote from German Philosopher, Arthur Schopenhauer: "the first forty years of life give us the text: the next thirty supply the commentary". Or a quotation from Benjamin Franklin, one of American's eighteenth-century scientist, politician and prolific writer: "At twenty years of age, the will reigns; at thirty, the wit; and at forty, the judgement".

Apart from the thought-provoking quotes, there are witty cartoons designed to generate laughter and produce satirical comments about one's progress or lack of it in one's lifetime. The musical monologue, *Life Begins at Forty*, performed by Russian-born American actress and singer, Sophie Tucker, the comedy, film and television series entitled *Life Begins at Forty* are examples of the attention given to age forty.

Although there is enough 'evidence' to suggest that life begins at forty, it did at forty-five for Sandra and her children. Every week, leading up to her final departure, she meticulously discussed with and explained to Patricia and little Judith the need to move out of the matrimonial home. She was very aware of the damage it could have on them, especially Patricia, who was progressing gradually from her emotional and physical difficulties. But were those long discussions enough? Did the discussion time help the girls to understand why they had to leave their childhood home? How would the children recapture the memories that are etched on the walls of their two-bedroom home? Would the move be pouring more combustible fuel into the already burning fire?

It was only a matter of time before the all-important question would arise.

"Mum, so where will we be living?" Patricia asked

"Cynthia said that we could come to hers for a few weeks until we got our own place," the decisive mother informed her.

"And all of this stuff?" Patricia asked, referring to the household items.

I will leave them here," mum declared.

While there seem to be a happy mood about moving house, I became concerned. All along, Sandra's main desire was to find total relief for her children's emotional, physical and psychological difficulties. Having arrived at this point, I wondered if she would be able to maintain the progress with Patricia's health.

The subject of leaving home is both scary and debatable. Some of us are eager to reach 16 or 18 so that we can leave the home of our carers, guardians or parents. We leave for various reasons such as going to university away from our home city or town, taking a job far away or migrating to another country. At times we are forced out because we display undesirable behaviour in the home and are forced out. Maybe we leave because of a heated and unresolved argument with a parent or sibling.

When I reflected on my own experience, I hadn't turned twenty-one fast enough before my maternal grandfather and I had heated arguments about using my money to purchase items to redecorate his house. Having just started to teach at a primary school, I decided to pay the utility bills-electricity, gas, telephone and water- since he was a pensioner. Unfortunately, my grandfather perceived that I was earning a huge salary and began making unplanned demands on my finances. He expected me to give him a monthly stipend for looking after me while I was at secondary school. He wanted funds to replace the furniture that I dismantled. And he wanted me to pay some of the maintenance workers whom he hired to carry out repairs to his house. Being youthful and inexperienced, I often responded to his unjust demands and inhumane threats.

About five months after, I came to the point when I resolved in my mind that I had had enough. I refused to take the constant verbal battering, the incessant reminders of my infanthood plight, and the continuous referral to my mother's illness. The one blow that pierced my heart was him reminding me of my sick mother. His words frequently plagued my thoughts since I performed all the house chores. My willingness to abandon him increased daily. I decided to pack my belongings: books, clothes and television and go to my mother's house. Since I did not have my own transportation, I telephoned one of my former secondary school teachers, with whom I still had contact and asked him if he could transport my stuff. He inquired about my reason for leaving. On relating to him my long struggle and ardent battle with my grandfather, he cautioned me to take a few days to rethink my decision because I may be 'jumping from the frying pan into the fire'.

The days had flown by rapidly, but time did not help. I could only envisage me leaving my boyhood home. Eventually, I secured another means of transportation and left the home where I spent twelve of the most precious years of my life. I contacted a colleague of mine with whom I was teaching and set the date. I waited until my grandfather would be away and then made my permanent exist. While the memories of my departure are still etched in my thoughts even today, I have no regrets because I felt I needed to be liberated.

Life is full of questions and with hindsight, they emerge. At times when things go wrong, we hope to remedy the situation by looking back. I pose the following questions to you: Have you been pinned down by circumstances? How did you respond? What resources did you draw on to aid you? In addressing your quest for liberation, who was at a disadvantage? Did you arrive at your decision gradually or suddenly? Did you regret gaining the freedom?

Turning back to this family's ordeal, being aware that Sandra was on the verge of leaving her matrimonial home, I felt the need to engage in proactive pastoral counselling. With the various battles and struggles that she had had not so long ago and with the challenges she would be facing soon, I believe a pastoral session would have benefited her. I called to enquire about her well-being.

"Hi Sandra," I greeted after telephoning.

"Oh, that's you. I am O.K. What about you?"

"I'm doing O.K also. How is it going?" I asked.

"Fairly O.K. Patricia is doing much better."

She sounded upbeat as though she was expecting a miracle in her life.

"How are you managing with the house hunting?" I asked

"I am still searching high and low," the hopeful mum replied.

"You know it will be challenging, especially to find affordable accommodation."

"Well, I went looking for accommodation today, but they are so expensive," she informed me.

"What are the prices like?" I asked.

"£600, 700 and £800. That's a lot. I don't know if I would be able to manage that kind of money," she replied.

"How are you feeling now that you have left home?" I inquired.

"I am coping much better and my mind is at ease. Thank you for helping us with the sessions with Sharon."

We hadn't finished speaking when Sandra heard a beep on her mobile phone.

"Let me call you back," she requested.

"Hello."

"Hello, Sandra. This is Janice's social worker. I want to alert you that we are reviewing Janice fostering progress. May I come over at 2 pm tomorrow and discuss some new developments with you?"

"Sure, I'll be here." The mother-of-three assured her.

My telephone rang. It was a delightful Sandra on the other end.

"Hi, It's me. That was the social worker. She wants to meet with me tomorrow."

"O.K. That's interesting. I trust that everything is O.K."

"Listen, I need to sort a few things out. Let me speak with you another time," Sandra requested.

The day had rushed by. At about 1:50 p.m the next day, Sandra had returned to the matrimonial home to check on her belongings and also to meet with the social worker. With the doorbell ringing, Sandra opened the door and greeted the social worker:

"Hi! Good afternoon. Come on in."

"Good afternoon."

Sandra invited the social worker to take a seat in the living room an offered her a drink.

"The time away from home helped Janice tremendously," the social worker shared.

"What does that mean?" Sandra asked.

"Looking at Janice progress, the department has decided to return her to you. We don't normally do this but we believe that you should have her back. But we will be monitoring you monthly," the social worker updated her.

"When will she be coming back?" Sandra asked, with a smile stretching across her face.

It was a cool evening, almost approaching the late hours of the day, when Jesus and His disciples were travelling approximately twenty-five miles, on foot, from Capernaum to Nain, a Galilean town, south-east of Nazareth. The many miracles which Jesus performed led to His popularity and so a massive crowd also joined in the trip to the Galilean town. Jesus' extensive ministry included, healing people of their physical ailments, teaching the words of life, providing spiritual healing for the souls of many and inspiring the emotionally-oppressed. By now the disciples must have been excited since Jesus had just healed a sick man. The scores of people who went on the trip were engrossed in vibrant conversations about the miracle which Jesus had just performed. In fact it was possible that they were wondering if they would witness more miracles before sunset.

On approaching the entrance to the woman's village, Jesus and his entourage encountered a funeral procession. A widow was on her way to the cemetery to lay her only son to rest. Being a widow, this mother's marital status very likely had hindered her from having the funds to hire professional mourners. Consequently, the women of the village most likely were leading the procession as they wept openly. In this Jewish society, widowhood brought loneliness and financial hardship. But a childless widow may even be worst off in this society. And there was the emotional and psychological impact, especially if the widow was poor.

The sight of the sorrowful weeping, the boisterous wailing, the grief-stricken faces and the huge crowd of mourners touched Jesus' heart to the point where he had compassion on the mournful mother. This event moved Jesus to offer sympathy to this widow from the inner parts, the seat of emotions. When this Miracle Worker encouraged the widow not to cry, he was implying indirectly that He had seen her wound, heard her plea and was eager to heal her.

As Jesus sympathetically touched the coffin, everything stopped. The pallbearers, the mourners only sobbed while standing still. Jesus, authoritatively commands the dead man to rise and without much fuss, handed him over to his weeping mother. Hardly expecting such a turn of events, the crowd gasped in awe and amazement, while the once-dead son sat up. In the midst of a situation where a community supported one of its members, we see comfort and healing being extended the marginalised and weak. This was visible evidence that life began for this lonely mother.

Returning to the conversation between the social worker and Sandra, the social worker alerted her:

"Well we need to give the foster parents ample time. It should be about seven to eight weeks."

"Oh! What a relief! I can have my family together again!" she exclaimed.

Afterwards, the social worker left. Sandra's heart bubbled. Her face lighted up. This was truly a case where *Life Begins at 45!* Soon after, my telephone rang. It was Sandra on the other end.

"Hi, it's me. Guess what?"

"You have a house."

"No. The social worker just told me that I am getting Janice back. Can you believe that?"

"Congratulations! Terrific! We give God thanks for that. No doubt you are jumping for joy," I replied.

"You can say that again. I thought I had lost her to the foster parents forever."

"No doubt you are looking forward to this. So when will she be coming home?" I added.

"I am really lifted up. It could be in the next 2 months."

"I'm happy for you. Let me call you later. I need to rush off," I quietly replied.

One week later, having found a lovely decorated house, Sandra called.

I picked up my mobile phone.

"Hello!"

"Hi! Guess what?" she asked with excitement in her voice.

"You have a job?" I asked.

"No. We found a house and it's really nice. I can move in any time," she alerted me.

"Brilliant. Wonderful. Congrats."

The God of Heaven has answered prayer. A few days later, Sandra and the girls began packing their stuff, in preparation for the removal van. She stripped the kitchen of its pots, pans, baking trays and other cooking utensils. In the living room, the piano, three-piece settee and most of the floral lamps were prepared for removal. And upstairs in the bedrooms, there were numerous suitcases full of clothes.

The following Tuesday, a white sixteen-wheeler removal truck pulled up outside her home. Two men jumped out of the vehicle, attached a platform to the truck's door and then rang the doorbell. On seeing Sandra appeared at the door, the driver asked her about the luggage that needed removing. Having cleared the walkway in the living room, they tackled all three chairs and left them outside the truck. They managed to remove all three sofas to the outside of the house. Since the long three-seater sofa would take more space than the other two smaller ones, the workers lifted it in and secure it tightly. As they appeared at the truck's door, torrential rain suddenly gushed from the heavens.

"Oh my word!" replied Steve, the driver.

"Get the plastic covering quickly," his partner ordered.

In the meantime, the water was soaking into the sofas' sponge and cloth. About three minutes after, Sandra rushed to the door in time to see her rain-soaked sofas. The workmen had spread the thick plastic covering over the two sofas and rushed into the house.

"Can these be covered by your company's insurance?" she asked firmly.

"I will have to report it to the manager when we return to the office," the driver replied.

"But don't you have insurance to cover these?" the other worker asked.

"I do, but I am not sure that it will cover this type of incident," Sandra added.

The dark clouds covered the sky. The rain continued to rain 'cats and dogs'. Suddenly, Steve looked through the window and noticed that the truck's door was left opened, causing the rain to wet the threshold of the door.

"Do you have a brollie?" he asked Sandra.

She quickly pulled one from behind the cloak rack in the walkway. Steve flipped it opened, rushed out, closed the door and simultaneously turned and headed back into the house. A few minutes after, the clouds slid away and the clear sky appeared again. During this time, the girls had been busy bringing the luggage from the bedrooms. The men immediately resumed their work. Within three hours they had packed everything into the truck and were ready to transport the household items to the new home.

Turning to the process of decision-making, you would agree that some decisions are harder to make than others. Then, they are decisions which are more important than others. However, whatever decision you are faced with, requires various skills and techniques. Good decision-making techniques involve identifying the problem to be solved, collecting information about the problem, identifying the standards to judge the solution by and evaluating the outcomes of your actions. Such techniques are needed for a career to be successful or for effective leadership to take place. Importantly, companies, which specialise in training individuals for leadership roles, have identified a number of tools which can assist individuals in good decision-making.

If there was ever a time that the term, *Life Begins at 45,* is appropriate, it was during this stage of Sandra's life. Janice had returned and took her place in the family again. The prospect of starting her career as a social worker was on the horizon. The opportunity to live in a new home and start a new life as a single-parent and be the lone breadwinner definitely were evidence that *Life Began at 45* for the serious, achievement-driven mother-of-three. Not to mention residing in a stable environment.

Taking a reflective look at Sandra's journey, we witness the strong support from her community, which contributed to this transformation. Our journeys may seem endless and it may bring struggles and mountainous hurdles which we seek to overcome. And along the path, we may have to face some open wounds. In the meantime, individuals may not hear our appeals: whether silent or loud. But when the love and compassion of God are demonstrated through members of our community, we experience the touch of God through human lives. And if you are at the stage in your life, you can echo the sentiments: *Life Begins at 45!*

**Thoughts for Action *[Jot down your responses]***

* Have you ever felt the need for freedom?

* What was that thing or person from which you wanted to be liberated: an abusive marriage, obsession, addiction, controlling habit, a frightening fear, guilt, a demanding individual or an unstable environment?

- What impact did it have on you?

- How did you handle it?

- Share what steps you took and how you benefitted.

- How can you use your experience to help someone who is searching for liberation?

**Moments of Surrender**

- Spend some time prayerfully reflecting on Galatians 5:2: "Stand fast therefore in the liberty by which Christ has made us free, and do not be entangled again with a yoke of bondage."

- Having reached this section of the book, to what extent have you truly experienced real freedom?

# EPILOGUE

# THE UNTHINKABLE

When we contemplate on the unthinkable, we imagine events and situations which are incapable of being done or considered. The unthinkable can hardly be achieved by someone. There is the idea of something being incredible, inconceivable or unimaginable or extremely improbable. When we hear of the word 'unthinkable', it creates imagines in our minds of something taking place in a way that is against logic and normal reasoning. Whether it is climbing Mount Everest or walking from one end of Niagara Falls to the other end on a tight rope, we consider such things to be the unthinkable.

A year later, Patricia was sitting in the living room of their new home, when suddenly she felt something dripping down her neck. She put her hands on it. The more she wiped it away, the more the sticky liquid flowed down her neck.

"Mummy! Mummy! Come quickly!" the startled teenager shouted fearfully.

Her mother rushed out of the kitchen and looked at the liquid which was dripping from her daughter's ears.

"This looks serious. I need to get you off to the doctors."

Since Patricia was dressed fairly well, mum slipped on a pullover and jumped into the car with Patricia following her. Meanwhile, she had asked Janice to babysit Judith.

"Why are my ears dripping? Will I be deaf? I don't want to be disabled," she responded tearfully.

Patricia's mother's face carried a mask of concerns. Her face bore the resemblance of a woman with deep questions. As she pushed the car with the accelerator, her thoughts were racing. They covered the half-mile distance to the medical centre in about three minutes. Having parked the car in the only available space, both of them jumped out and rushed into the doctors' surgery. Mum approached the receptionist and explained the situation.

"Let me see who is available," the receptionist replied.

"The Otolaryngologist, says he will see you now. Take a left here and go straight ahead."

Patricia and her mother walked briskly along the hallway.

"What is an otolaryngologist?" Patricia enquired.

"He is a doctor who specializes in problems with the ears, nose and throat," her mother replied.

The anxious mother-of-three, on see the doctor's name was about to knock on the varnished door when the doctor opened it and beckoned for them to join him.

"What can I do for you?" he asked

With Patricia still wiping the dripping liquid from her neck intermittently, her mother explained what had happened. The doctor looked at Patricia's ears,

He took his autoscope and peered into her ears. Looking a bit concerned, he checked his computer for Patricia's file.

"You were diagnosed for Tinnitus."

He checked her ears again and then explained that part of her problem seemed to be an ear infection and that this was the reason for the dripping.

"Let me see if I can get you some medication to clear your ears and at the same time make an appointment for you to see the audiologist."

He delicately took up his pink appointment sheets, filled it out and then hand it over to Patricia, instructing her to hand it to the receptionist so that an appointment can be made to see the audiologist. They left the room and headed for the receptionist. Afterwards, they went over to the pharmacy to get the medication.

Two weeks later, Patricia and her mother attended the audiologist. By this time the dripping had stopped. He briefly reviewed her medical noted and then tested her ears. He verified whether she could hear well and also how much noise she could endure. To his amazement, Patricia seemed not to be affected by any noise. Actually, she was given the all clear from the Tinnitus. What thrilling news! There was a sense of relief on their faces. The daily battle was over. Life had taken a turn for the better for Patricia. Her mother was experiencing answers to prayer.

This terrific medical news provided the opportunity for Patricia to return to school on a regular basis. On successfully completed her GCSEs with excellent grades, went on to Sixth Form to pursue 'A' Levels. By this time, Patricia's middle sister, Janice, had resettled with her family, her behavior had improved tremendously and she was attending school regularly and performing well. Patricia's mother, having secured a more peaceful environment for her children, regained her mental stability and was able to resume her training as a social worker. Meanwhile, the sessions with the speech therapist along with her involvement in various speech programmes assisted Judith in progressing with her speech problem. Unfortunately, Patricia's dad was re-admitted to the psychiatric institution indefinitely because of his deteriorating mental condition. This family was experiencing the unthinkable. Their open wounds were closed. Such events bring families closer and they certainly kept this family together in spite of the many challenges. It is evident that even though we may have wounds, it's the faith in the God of Heaven and the care from your community that aid us in experiencing healing.

When we consider the unthinkable, we must admit that since it is beyond our human resources, it can only be because of the divine touch, spiritual guidance and prayer. We see the God of Heaven working through the ebbs and flows of this ordinary family to provide comfort, healing and restoration. Although we often cry out to our fellow human beings for help, it is even more powerful when we can reach out to God who responds to families' desperate pleas. The power of prayer is awesome, especially when we are confronted with the impossible or the unthinkable. Would you not want to bask excitedly in that moment when God is *Raising the Wounded* and you could be one of them!

# NOTES

1   William H. Willimon, *Pastor: The Theology and Practice of Ordained Ministry* (Nashville: Abingdon Press, 2002), p.58.

2   William H. Willimon, *Pastor,* p.58.

3   Schlachter, A., "Virtiligo: Overcoming from Cuba the Stranger" http://www.deltapimuzik.com/vitiligo/melagininaplus.htm

4   Samuel Bacchiocchi, *Divine Rest for Human Restlessness: A Theological Study of the Good News of the Sabbath for Today* (Michigan: Biblical Perspectives, 2001), p. 79.

5   Ross P. Scherer, "Wellness" in *Encyclopedia of Religion and Society,* Ed. William H. Swatos, Jr., (London: SAGE Publications, 1998), pp. 554-556 (555).

6   Malcolm H. Schvey, "Tinnitus" in *Collier's Encyclopedia,* Ed. B Johnston. (New York: P. F Collier, 1994), Vol. 22, p.331..

7   Bacchiocchi, *Divine Rest for Human Restlessness*, p. 62.

8   Francis, D. Nichol, *The Seventh-day Adventist Bible Commentary* (Maryland: Review & Herald, 2005), vol. 1, p.223.

9   Ellen G. White, *Adventist Home (*Nashville, Southern Publishing, 1952), p.25.

10  Francis Martin, "Gift of Healing", in *The New International Dictionary of Pentecostal and Charismatic Movements, rev and exp edn.,* Eds. Stanley M. Burgess and Eduard M. van der Maas (Michigan: Zondervan, 2002), pp. 694-698 (694).

11  Nichol, *The Seventh-day Adventist Bible Commentary,* p.223.

12  Additional Old Testament references can be found in Deuteronomy 7:15; 32:39;

Psalms 6:2-3;30:2;41:4;103:3;147:3;Isaiah 30:26; 53:5. A New Testament referenceis seen in 1 Peter 2:24.

[13] These texts also provide a summary of Jesus' healing ministry as seen in Mt. 8:16-17;9:35-36;14:34-36;15:29-31.

[14] Scherer, "Wellness", p.554.

[15] Neil J. Twombly, "Prayer" in *Collier's Encyclopedia*. Ed. B. Johnston. (New York: P. F Collier,1994), Vol. 19, p.314.

[16] John Hospers, "Miracles" in *Collier's Encyclopedia*. Ed. B. Johnston. (New York: P. F Collier,1994), Vol. 16, p 345-348 (345).

[17] Hospers, "Miracles", p. 345.

[18] Martin, "Gift of Miracles", p.876.

[19] W. H. Mare, "1 Corinthians" in *The Expositor's Bible Commentary,* Ed. F. E. Gaebelein (London: Pickering & Inglis, Vol. 10, 1976), pp. 173-298 (262).

[20] Craig A. Evans "Mark", in *Commentary on the Bible*, Ed. James D. G. Dunn and John W. Rogerson, (Michigan: Eerdmans, 2003), p. 1079.

[21] Bonnie B. Thurnstone, *Preaching Mark (*Minneapolis: Fortress Press, 2002), p.75.

[22] Paul Avis, *A Ministry Shaped by Mission* (London: T & T Clark, 2005), Pp. 60-61.

[23] Derek Tidball, *Skilful Shepherds: Explorations in Pastoral* Theology (Leicester: Apollos, 1997), p.292.

[24] Ernest Lucas & Peter May, "The Significance of Jesus' Healing Ministry" in *Christian Healing: What Can We Believe?*, Ed. Ernest Lucas, (London: SPCK, 1997), pp.85-108, (99).

[25] Stephen C. Barton, "1 Corinthians", in *Commentary on the Bible*, Eds. James D. G. Dunn and John W. Rogerson, (Michigan: Eerdmans, 2003), pp. (1314-1352) 1341.

[26] Martin, "Gift of Healing", p. 696.

[27] Of the three other conclusions that Martin has arrived at, he is of the view that God brings about healing through the ministry of elders and the prayer of faith. See F. Martin, "Gift of Healing", p. 697.

[28] For an in-depth classification of these two Protestant movements, see David

B. Barrett & Todd M. Johnson, "Global Statistics" in *The New International Dictionary of Pentecostal and Charismatic Movements,* rev and exp edn, Eds. Stanley M. Burgess & Eduard M. Van der Mass, (Michigan: Zondervan, 2002), pp. 286-287.

29   Seventh-day Adventist World Statistics", http://www.adventist.org/world-church/facts-and-figures/index.html [Accessed August 2010].

30   Lawrence E. Sullivan, "Healing", in *The Encyclopedia of Religion,* Eds. Charles J. Adams, Joseph M. Kitagawa et al., vol. 6, (New York: Macmillan Publishing, 1987), pp. 226-234 (226).

31   Robert M. Anderson, "Pentecostal and Charismatic Christianity" in *Encyclopedia of Religion and Society,* Ed. William H. Swatos, Jr., (London: SAGE Publications, 1998), pp. 229-235 (230).

32   Anderson, "Pentecostal and Charismatic Christianity" p. 231.

33   Anderson, "Pentecostal and Charismatic Christianity", p. 232.

34   David B. Barrett & Todd M. Johnson, "Global Statistics" in *The New International Dictionary of Pentecostal and Charismatic Movements,* rev and exp edn, Eds. Stanley M. Burgess & Eduard M. Van der Mass, (Michigan: Zondervan, 2002), pp. 283-302 (293).

35   Sullivan, "Healing", p. 233.

36   Cecil M. Robeck, Jr., "Pentecostalism" in *The Oxford Companion to Christian Thought,* Eds. Adrian Hastings, Alistair Mason and Hugh Pyper (Oxford: Oxford University Press, 2000), pp. 530-532 (531).

37   Cecil M. Robeck, Jr., "Pentecostalism", p. 531.

38   Frank D. Macchia, "Pentecostal Theology" in *The New International Dictionary of Pentecostal and Charismatic Movements, rev and exp edn.,* Eds. Stanley M. Burgess and Eduard M. van der Maas (Michigan: Zondervan, 2002), pp. 1120-1141 (1135).

39   Alistair Mason, "Charismatic Movement" in *The Oxford Companion to Christian Thought,* Eds. Adrian Hastings, Alistair Mason and Hugh Pyper (Oxford: Oxford University Press, 2000), pp.107-108 (107). For a discussion on the term evangelical and its definitions, see Roger E. Olson, *The SCM Press A-Z of Evangelical Theology* (London: SCM Press, 2005), pp 3-6. In David

Yamane, "Charismatic Movement", in *Encyclopedia of Religion and Society,* Ed. William H. Swatos, Jr., (London: SAGE Publications, 1998), pp. 80-82, the author shares a brief overview of the Charismatics' history and origin.

[40] Stephen Hunt, "Charismatic Movements" in *Encyclopedia of New Religious Movements,* Ed. Peter B. Clarke (London: Routledge, 2006), pp. 95-97 (96). See also E. A. Livingstone (Ed.), *The Oxford Dictionary of the Christian Church,* 3rd edn (Oxford: Oxford University Press, 2005), p. 324.

[41] Peter D. Hocken, "Charismatic Movement" in *The New International Dictionary of Pentecostal and Charismatic Movements, rev and exp edn.,* (Eds.) Stanley M. Burgess and Eduard M. van der Maas (Michigan: Zondervan, 2002), pp. 477-519 (515).

[42] George W. Reid, "Health and Healing" in *Handbook of Seventh-day Adventist Theology,* Eds. George W. Reid and Raoul Dederen (Maryland: Review and Herald Publishing Association, 2000), pp 751-783 (760).

[43] Reid, "Health and Healing", p.766.

[44] Reid, "Health and Healing", p.766.

[45] Reid, "Health and Healing", p.771.

[46] Wesley Carr, *Handbook of Pastoral Studies: Learning and Practising Christian Ministry* (London: SPCK, 1997), p.9.

[47] Wesley Carr, *Handbook of Pastoral Studies,* p. 11. In F. Martin, "Gift of Healing" p. 694, the author expands further on the concept of shalom by providing a transliteration indicating that it means the presence in a person or a relationship, of all that ought to be there.

[48] Apart from healing, the Church has traditionally been involved in four other tasks: sustaining, reconciling, nurturing and guiding. For a comprehensive discussion of these tasks see William A. Clebsch and Charles R. Jaekle, *Pastoral Care in Historical Perspective* (NY: Jason Aronson, 1983), pp. 33-66

[49] Graham Dow & Trevor Stammers, "The Church's Ministry of Healing Today" in *Christian Healing: What Can We Believe?,* Ed. Ernest Lucas, (London: SPCK, 1997), pp.31-58, (36).

[50] Dow & Stammers, "The Church's Ministry of Healing Today", p.39.

[51] Nigel Wright & Sheila Smith, "Suffering" in *Christian Healing: What Can We*

*Believe?*, Ed. Ernest Lucas, (London: SPCK, 1997), pp.120-121. (109-139).

[52] Tidball, *Skilful Shepherds,* p. 292.

[53] Other psalmodic expressions of the 'waiting' motif can be found in Ps. 52.9; 62:1,5;69:3,9;104:27;123:2;130:6. These verses indicate that the psalmist was expecting God to come to his rescue, knowing that there was no one else on whom he could depend.

[54] Willem S. Prinsloo, "The Psalms", in *Commentary on the Bible*, Eds. James D. G. Dunn and John W. Rogerson, (Michigan: Eerdmans, 2003), pp. (364-436) 366.

[55] Ibid

[56] Prinsloo, "The Psalms", p.367.

[57] Prinsloo, "The Psalms", p.374.

[58] Martin, "Gift of Healing", p.698.

[59] Ray S. Anderson, *The Soul of Ministry: Forming Leaders of God's People* (Kentucky: Westminster John Knox Press, 1997), p. 174

[60] Martin, "Gift of Healing", p.696.

[61] Martin, "Gift of Healing", p.697.

[62] Lucy Tobin, "South Africa's Children Caring for Parents with Aids", *The Guardian,* June 2010, http://www.guardian.co.uk/education/2010/jun/22/hiv-aids-child-carers-south-africa [Accessed August, 2010]. Revised and adapted.

[63] Ellen G. White, *Prophets and Kings (*Nashville, Tennessee: Southern Publishing, 1917), p.102.

[64] Jesus' ministry made Him famous among the Galileans and people from many other geographical areas. See Mt. 4:24-25; 8:16-17;9:35-36; 14:34-36;15:29-31.

[65] Anthony J. Saldarini, "Matthew", in *Commentary on the Bible*, Eds. James D. G. Dunn and John W. Rogerson, (Michigan: Eerdmans, 2003), p. 1012.

[66] Saldarini, "Matthew", p. 1012.

[67] Ernest Lucas noted that contemporary Christian believers have been demonstrating a keen interest in health and healing, in that this interest stemmed from the fact that healing was a central feature in Jesus' ministry. See Ernest Lucas, "Introduction" in *Christian Healing: What Can We Believe?*, Ed. Ernest Lucas, (London: SPCK, 1997), p.1. (1-4)

[68]  This theological theme is pervasive in the Synoptic Gospels Mk 1.14-15, Mt 4.23; 9.35, Lk 17.20-21. However, Lucas and May were quick to remark that although this theme was central to Jesus' preaching, he did not give a specific definition for it. See Ernest Lucas & Peter May, "The Significance of Jesus' Healing Ministry" in *Christian Healing: What Can We Believe?*, Ed. Ernest Lucas, (London: SPCK, 1997), (85-108) p.88. Stephen Pattison highlights a similar view on the Kingdom of God. See Pattison, "Health and Healing", p. 286.

[69]  Lucas & May, "The Significance of Jesus' Healing Ministry", p. 91. Pattison also echoes the same sentiments. See Pattison, "Health and Healing", p. 285 and F. Martin, "Gift of Healing", p. 696.

[70]  Walter Wink, *The Engaging Powers: Discernment and Resistance in a World of Domination* (Minneapolis: Fortress Press, 1992), p. 134

[71]  Pattison, "Health and Healing", p. 285.

[72]  Avis, *A Ministry Shaped by Mission,* p.78.

[73]  Dow & Stammers, "The Church's Ministry of Healing Today", p.48.

[74]  , Ellen G. White, *Medical Ministry* (Boise, Idaho: Pacific Press Publication Association, 1932), p. 16.

[75]  RMS Titanic, http://en.wikipedia.org/wiki/RMS_Titanic [Accessed August, 2010]. Revised and adapted.

[76]  Herman Ridderbos, *The Gospel According to John: A Theological Commentary* (Grand Rapis, Michigan: William B. Eerdmans Publishing Company, 1997), p.545.

[77]  Ridderbos, *The Gospel According to John,* p.545.

[78]  In Joel 3:10; 2 Corinthian 12:10 and Hebrews 12:2, Yahweh indicates His concerns for the Weak also.

[79]  Babette Rothschild, *The Body Remembers: The Psychophysiology of Trauma and Trauma Treatment* (New York: W. W. Norton & Company, 2000), p.5.

[80]  Rothschild, *The Body Remembers,* p.6.

[81]  George Muller & Diana L. Matisko, *The Autobiography of George Muller* (Pennsylvania: Whitaker House, 1985), pp. 11-12.

[82]  See the full story in *A Journey of the Bold and the Young: Living on the Edge.*

[83] In Acts 19:11-12, the Apostle Paul engaged in a method similar to that described in Acts 5:12-16, in that aprons and handkerchiefs which were put on Paul's body, were used to heal the sick.

[84] Michael Perham, *New Handbook of Pastoral Liturgy* (London: SPCK, 2000), p.189.

[85] Perham, *New Handbook of Pastoral Liturgy*, p.191.

[86] John T. Squires, "Acts", in *Commentary on the Bible*, Eds. James D. G. Dunn and John W. Rogerson, (Michigan: Eerdmans, 2003), pp.1213 – 1267 (1223).

[87] Ellen G. White, *Counsels on Health* (Mountain View, California: Pacific Press,1923), p.34.

[88] White, *Counsels on Health*, p. 210.

[89] Kate Litchfield, *Tend My Flock: Sustaining Good Pastoral Care* (London: Canterbury Press, 2006), p.15.

[90] Litchfield, *Tend My Flock*, p.16.

[91] Squires, "Acts", p. 1235.

[92] Dow & Stammers, "The Church's Ministry of Healing Today", p.45.

[93] Dow & Stammers, "The Church's Ministry of Healing Today", p.48.

[94] Steven Croft, *Ministry in Three Dimensions: Ordination and Leadership in the Local Church* (London: Darton, Lognman & Todd Ltd, 1999), p.132.

[95] Gary Collins, *Christian Counseling: A Comprehensive Guide, rev. edn.* (Dallas, TX: Word Publishing, 1988), p. 44

[96] Collins, *Christian Counseling*, p.135.

[97] For a full discussion on the two categories of guilt (objective and subjective), see Collins, *Christian Counseling*, pp.135-136.

[98] See R. Gross and R. McIlveen, *Psychology: A New Introduction* (London: Hodder & Stoughton, 1998), p. 413 for a discussion of Eric Erikson's eight stages of psychosocial development, with intimacy versus isolation being one of these stages.

[99] Litchfield, *Tend My Flock*, p.106.

[100] Perham, *New Handbook of Pastoral Liturgy*, p.190

[101] Perham, *New Handbook of Pastoral Liturgy*, p.191.

[102] Litchfield, *Tend My Flock*, p.13.